Series / Number 07-060

LINEAR PROGRAMMING
An Introduction

BRUCE R. FEIRING
University of Minnesota

SAGE PUBLICATIONS
The International Professional Publishers
Newbury Park   London   New Delhi

I wish to thank my family for their patience.

For information address:

SAGE Publications, Inc.
275 South Beverly Drive
Beverly Hills, California 90212

SAGE Publications India Pvt. Ltd.
M-32 Market
Greater Kailash I
New Delhi 110 048 India

SAGE Publications Ltd
28 Banner Street
London EC1Y 8QE
England

International Standard Book Number 0-8039-2850-5

Library of Congress Catalog Card No. 85-082647

THIRD PRINTING, 1990

When citing a university paper, please use the proper form. Remember to cite the correct
Sage University Paper series title and include the paper number. One of the following
formats can be adapted (depending on the style manual used):

(1) IVERSEN, GUDMUND R. and NORPOTH, HELMUT (1976) "Analysis of
Variance." Sage University Paper series on Quantitative Applications in the Social
Sciences, 07-001. Beverly Hills: Sage Pubns.

OR

(2) Iversen, Gudmund R. and Norpoth, Helmut. 1976. *Analysis of Variance.* Sage
University Paper series on Quantitative Applications in the Social Sciences, series no.
07-001. Beverly Hills: Sage Pubns.

CONTENTS

Series Editor's Introduction   5

1. Introduction   7

2. Linear Programming Modeling   12

3. Graphical Solution of Linear Programs in
   Two Variables   28

4. The Simplex Method for Solving Linear Programs   32

   Standard Form   32
   Solving Systems of Linear Equations and Terminology   34
   Principles of the Simplex Method   37
   General Basic Steps of the Simplex Method   37
   Condition for Optimality   41
   Summary of the Simplex Method (Basic Steps
      for a Maximization Problem)   41
   The Simplex Method in Tableau Form   42
   Finding a Feasible Basis   46
   The Big M Simplex Method (or Method
      of Penalty)   47

5. Sensitivity (or Postoptimality) Analysis   50

   Changes in the Objective Coefficients
      (Objective Function Coefficient Ranging)   51
   Changes in the Resources (Right-Hand-Side
      Constants)   54

6. Computer Solutions to Linear Programming Problems   59

   Input   59
   Output   62

Appendix 1: Properties of Linear Programming Problems   69

    Convex Sets   69
    Hyperplanes   70
    Feasible Solutions   71
    Optimal Feasible Solutions   73
    Development of the Simplex Algorithm   77
    Changing a Basis Vector—Feasibility   77
    Changing the Objective Function—Optimality   79

**Appendix 2: Linear Programming Methods for
Production Scheduling   81**

    Asset Management Control Policies   82
    The Production Smoothing Model   83
    The Fixed Workforce Model   84
    The Variable Workforce Model   85

References   89

About the Author   91

Series Editor's Introduction

A large number of applications of linear programming are to be found in economics, business and industrial situations, engineering, statistics, and applied mathematics. Many of the examples in this book are of this type. New applications are beginning to appear with greater frequency in such fields as political science, psychology, sociology, and anthropology. We hope, through the publication of this monograph, to stimulate this trend and to encourage social scientists to add this methodology to their training and to use it whenever it is appropriate to their substantive and theoretical problems.

This monograph introduces the reader to linear programming in Chapter 1; discusses linear programming modeling concepts and examples in Chapter 2; provides a discussion of graphical solutions to lay a conceptual foundation for subsequent concepts in Chapter 3; presents the simplex method for solving linear problems in Chapter 4, carefully develops a solution procedure and provides economic interpretation by discussing sensitivity analysis in Chapter 5; and, finally, discusses computer linear programming codes for understanding input and output of commercially available LP codes in Chapter 6. The discussion provides the novice with the ability to model, solve, and analyze appropriate problems that lend themselves to linear programming methodologies. The Appendices provide a more rigorous mathematical development of basic linear programming properties. After the Appendices the reader will find a selected list of excellent references that discuss further the topics presented herein, and that build upon those topics.

The author provides a list of problems that are directly related to the discussion herein, and for which the solution will be clear. We advise the novice to work through these problems in order to understand the material more fully. Dr. Feiring developed this monograph from his class notes, suitably modified, and so it is in a sense already classroom tested. He has done an excellent job of making the material accessible to

6

those without an extensive quantitative background and of presenting the material for the general reader.

—*John L. Sullivan*
Series Co-Editor

LINEAR PROGRAMMING: AN INTRODUCTION

BRUCE R. FEIRING
University of Minnesota

1. INTRODUCTION

In 1947, George B. Dantzig discovered the Simplex Method for solving a large class of optimization problems known as linear programming problems. The term "programming" in the 1940s was synonymous with "planning." At that time, the word "programming" was not used to describe the development of computer code. In fact, Dantzig has acknowledged the contributions made by Nobel laureate (for economics) Koopmans and the great mathematician John von Neumann (who related linear programming to game theory).

Linear programming is a subset of mathematical programming, and the latter field is part of operations research. The following points are true of operations research:

(1) Alternatives or choices exist.

(2) Solutions are measured according to the attainment of specific objectives or criteria.

(3) Optimization, selection of the best alternative as measured by a stated criterion, is involved.

(4) Systems view—for example, considering interrelationships between components rather than separately—is involved.

In several studies of the comparative use of operations research methods, linear programming is usually first or second on the list. Other operations research techniques include simulation, network analysis, queuing theory, stochastic processes, dynamic programming, regression analysis, nonlinear programming, and game theory. Some of the real-world production applications of linear programming are in production scheduling, production planning and repair, plant layout, equipment acquisition and replacement, blending, logistics, and plant location. In addition, many other applications from other areas exist as well.

Linear programming is a subset of mathematical programming that is concerned with the efficient allocation of limited resources to known activities with the objective of meeting a desired goal, such as maximizing profit or minimizing cost. The linearity of some models can be justified on the basis of physical properties of the problem. Some other nonlinear models can be linearized by the proper use of mathematical transformations.

Linear programming is a specific class of mathematical programming problem that satisfies the following conditions:

(1) The *decision variables* (unknowns) are nonnegative (positive or zero), that is, $X_i \geq 0$.

(2) The *criterion (objective function or performance index)* for choosing the "best" (optimal) values of the decision variables is a linear function of the decision variables, that is, a mathematical function of the form

$$Z = C_1 X_1 + C_2 X_2 + \ldots + C_n X_n = \sum_{i=1}^{n} C_i X_i$$

that involves only first powers of the variables, X_i, with no cross products.

(3) The *constraints* (operating rules) that govern the process can be expressed as linear equations and/or linear inequalities written in terms of the decision variables.

Conditions 2 and 3 justify the word "linear" in linear programming.

As indicated above, linear programming procedures are utilized widely to analyze numerous economic, social, military, and industrial (production) problems. Three main reasons for the wide use of linear programming are the following:

(1) A large variety of problems from diverse areas can either be represented or approximated as linear programming models.

(2) Efficient methods for solving linear programming problems are available.

(3) Sensitivity analysis allows for variation of problem data as an extension of the solution procedure for linear programming problems.

As the solution procedures for linear programming are iterative, most linear programming problems need to be solved by a computer. With the advance of computer hardware and linear programming software, the computer solution of large linear programming problems is fast and inexpensive.

Example 1. The following is a linear programming problem:

$$\text{maximize } Z = 3X_1 + 5X_2$$
$$\text{subject to} \quad X_1 + X_2 \leqslant 3$$
$$2X_1 + 3X_2 \leqslant 9$$
$$X_1 \geqslant 0, \ X_2 \geqslant 0$$

Note that the decision variables X_1 and X_2 are nonnegative (greater than or equal to zero). The objective function $Z = 3X_1 + 5X_2$, to be maximized, is written as linear function of the decision variables, and 3 and 5 are the *objective function coefficients*. The inequalities

$$X_1 + X_2 \leqslant 3$$
$$2X_1 + 3X_2 \leqslant 9$$

are the two constraints. The right-hand sides of the constraints (the numbers 3 and 9) are also called *resources*.

PROBLEMS

(1) Graph the two constraints (along with $X_1 \geq 0$, $X_2 \geq 0$) in two dimensions.

(2) On the same graph as in problem 1, graph the objective function (as a dotted line) when $Z = 3$, $Z = 5$, and $Z = 13$; that is, graph the three parallel lines L_1, L_2, L_3, where

$$L_1: \quad 3 = 3X_1 + 5X_2$$
$$L_2: \quad 5 = 3X_1 + 5X_2$$
$$L_3: \quad 13 = 3X_1 + 5X_2$$

(3) From your graph in problems 1 and 2, try to determine the values of X_1 and X_2 that satisfy the constraints that give the largest value of Z. (Look ahead to Chapters 2 and 3 if necessary.)

Note: In problem 1 above, to graph the constraint $X_1 + X_2 \leq 3$, first graph the line $X_1 + X_2 = 3$ (the graph of $X_1 + X_2 \leq 3$ is called a *closed half-space*). Recall that in graphing a line, two points determine a line, so select two convenient points that satisfy $X_1 + X_2 = 3$. For example, set $X_1 = 0$, so that $X_2 = 3$ [and we have the point $(X_1, X_2) = (0, 3)$]; set $X_2 = 0$, so that $X_1 = 3$ [and we have the point $(3, 0)$; also, some other points satisfying this equation are $(1, 2)$ and $(2, 1)$]. To find a point satisfying $X_1 + X_2 \leq 3$, use a test point such as $(1, 1)$. Observe that $1 + 1 = 2 < 3$. Another test point $(2, 2)$ has $2 + 2 = 4 > 3$, so that $(2, 2)$ does not satisfy $X_1 + X_2 \leq 3$. Thus, the graph of $X_1 + X_2 \leq 3$ consists of the line $X_1 + X_2 = 3$ as well as $X_1 + X_2 < 3$; that is, the line and below the line as shown in Figure 1.1.

Next, graph the closed half-space $2X_1 + 3X_2 \leq 9$ in the same manner on the same coordinate system. In order to find the point of intersection (an *extreme point* or corner point) of $X_1 + X_2 = 3$ and $2X_1 + 3X_2 = 9$, solve these equations simultaneously; that is, solve the system

$$X_1 + X_2 = 3$$
$$2X_1 + 3X_2 = 9$$

for X_1 and X_2. From elementary algebra, verify that the point of intersection $(X_1, X_2) = (0, 3)$. Next, in order to anticipate some of the modeling concepts of Chapter 2, consider the following simple model, called a *diet problem.*

Example 2. A dietitian is planning a menu that consists of two main foods: food A and food B. Each ounce of food A contains 2 units of fat, 1 unit of carbohydrate, and 4 units of protein. Each ounce of food B contains 2 units of fat, 3 units of carbohydrates, and 3 units

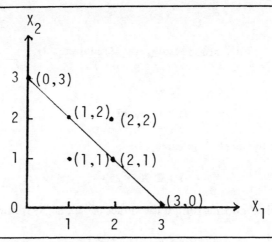

Figure 1.1: Graph of Constraint $X_1 + X_2 \leqslant 3$

of protein. The dietitian wants the meal to provide at least 18 units of fat, at least 12 units of carbohydrate, and at least 24 units of protein. If food A costs 20 cents per ounce and food B costs 25 cents per ounce, then how many ounces of each food should be served to minimize the cost of the meal and satisfy the dietitian's requirements?

Note: Much more complicated diet problems have been modeled as linear (or goal) programming models in many situations. One notable application has been to analyze Third World hunger problems by mathematical programming.

Let X_1 = number of ounces of food A that is served, and

X_2 = number of ounces of food B that is served.

Now, the number of units of fat contained in the meal is $2X_1 + 3X_2$, so that X_1 and X_2 need to satisfy

$$2X_1 + 3X_2 \geq 18 \text{ (fat requirement)}$$

Similarly, verify that

$$X_1 + 3X_2 \geq 12 \text{ (carbohydrate requirement)}$$

12

and

$$4X_1 + 3X_2 \geq 24 \text{ (protein requirement)}$$

where

$$X_1 \geq 0 \text{ and } X_2 \geq 0$$

The cost of the meal, Z, in cents, is

$$Z = 20X_1 + 25X_2$$

Thus, our diet model is to find the values of X_1 and X_2 that will

$$\text{minimize } Z = 20X_1 + 25X_2$$
$$\text{subject to} \quad 2X_1 + 3X_2 \geq 18$$
$$X_1 + 3X_2 \geq 12$$
$$4X_1 + 3X_2 \geq 24$$
$$X_1 \geq 0, \ X_2 \geq 0$$

PROBLEM

Graph the constraints and estimate the minimum cost that satisfies all of the constraints.

For more applications of operations research, see Wagner (1975), Hillier and Lieberman (1975), or Taha (1975, 1982). Also, these references provide a good list of application of linear programming in particular.

2. LINEAR PROGRAMMING MODELING

Three *basic steps* in constructing a linear programming model are as follows:

(1) Identify the *decision variables* (unknowns or independent variables). This step must be done first, as steps 2 and 3 depend on

step 1. In step 2 the constraints (operating rules), and in step 3 the objective function (criterion or performance index), will be written as a linear combination (e.g., in two dimensions, the graph is a straight line of the form ax + by) of the decision variables. Good modeling practice includes the use of the units of measurement (e.g., gallons/hour) when the decision variables are defined.

(2) Identify the *constraints* and write them as linear equations or inequalities in terms of the decision variables (from step 1).

(3) Identify the *objective function* and write it as a linear function of the decision variables.

The order of steps 2 and 3 is a decision to be determined by the individual modeler and may well depend upon how difficult the modeling exercise is to the modeler. Good modeling practice includes checking that terms to be added have the same units (you are not adding "apples and oranges"). Furthermore, for constraints, verify that the units on the left-hand side of the constraint are the same as the units on the right-hand side (resources); that is, check that you are not *comparing* apples to oranges. Another good practice in modeling is to write down, in words, what the objective function represents (e.g., total daily profit in dollars per day) and what *each* constraint represents (e.g., Los Angeles weekly demand constraint in tons per week). Further, a requirement of the solution procedure of linear programming (called the Simplex Method) is that all decision variables are nonnegative.

Example 1. A company has two grades of inspectors (1 and 2) who are to be assigned to an incoming quality control inspection for a high-volume part number. It is required that at least 1800 components to be inspected per 8-hour day. Grade 1 inspectors can check components at the rate of 25 per hour with an accuracy of 98%. Grade 2 inspectors check at the rate of 15 components per hour, with an accuracy of 95%.

The wage rate of a grade 1 inspector is $4.00 per hour, whereas that of a Grade 2 inspector is $3.00 per hour. Each time an error is made by an inspector, the cost to the company is $2.00. The company has available 8 grade 1 inspectors and 10 grade 2 inspectors for the inspection job. The company wants to determine the optimal (best) assignment of inspectors that will minimize the total cost of inspection.

FORMULATION

(1) *Decision variables:* The company needs to determine how many inspectors of each grade to assign to the job. Thus, let

X_1 = number of grade 1 inspectors to assign to the job, and

X_2 = number of grade 2 inspectors to assign to the job.

(2) *Constraints:* The company assigns *at most* (up to, no more than) 8 grade 1 inspectors such that:

$X_1 \leq 8$ (supply constraint for grade 1 inspectors) and, similarly

$X_2 \leq 10$ (supply constraint for grade 2 inspectors).

Also, it is required that *at least* 1800 components be inspected each day (by *both* types of inspectors):

$$(25 \text{ components/hour) (8 hours/day)} X_1 +$$
$$(15 \text{ components/hour) (8 hours/day)} X_2 \geq (1800 \text{ components/day)}$$

Note: 200 components/day are inspected by a *single* grade 1 inspector and $200 X_1$ components/day are inspected by *all* grade 1 inspectors. Similarly, $120 X_2$ components/day are inspected by *all* grade 2 inspectors. Thus,

$$200 X_1 + 120 X_2 \geq 1800$$

and dividing each term by 40 (to "scale" constraints in the above constraint; see note 2, example 8, this chapter)

$$5 X_1 + 3 X_2 \geq 45$$

represents that at least 1800 components are inspected each 8-hour day. Also,

$$X_1 \geq 0, \ X_2 \geq 0$$

means that the company will not hire a negative number of inspectors of each grade.

(3) *Objective function:* The total daily cost of inspection is modeled by the company (it desired to determine the values of X_1 and X_2; that is, the number of grade 1 and 2 inspectors to hire, to minimize this cost). First, observe that the hourly cost of one grade 1 inspector is

$$\$4/hr + (.02 \text{ error/component})(\$2/\text{error})(25 \text{ components/hr}) = \$5/hr$$

that is, the hourly wage plus the hourly cost of errors. Similarly, check that hourly cost of one grade 2 inspector is $\$4.50/hr$. Thus,

$$5X_1 + 4.5X_2$$

is the total *hourly* cost to the company and

$$Z = 40X_1 + 36X_2$$

is the total daily cost.

Summarizing, the company wants to determine X_1 and X_2 to

$$\text{minimize } Z = 40X_1 + 36X_2 \text{ (total daily cost in dollars per day)}$$

$$\text{subject to} \quad X_1 \leqslant 8 \text{ (grade 1 limitation)}$$

$$X_2 \leqslant 10 \text{ (grade 2 limitation)}$$

$$5X_1 + 3X_2 \geqslant 45 \text{ (at least 1800 pieces/day)}$$

$$X_1 \geqslant 0, \ X_2 \geqslant 0 \text{ (nonnegativity)}$$

Example 2. Once the analyst has modeled the previous problem in linear programming form, the next step is to solve for the unknowns. Because example 1 has only two decision variables, it is possible to solve this problem graphically (this would not be possible if there were four or more grades of inspectors).

As there are two variables, the problem is in two dimensions, and, by nonnegativity, the solution is in the first quadrant.

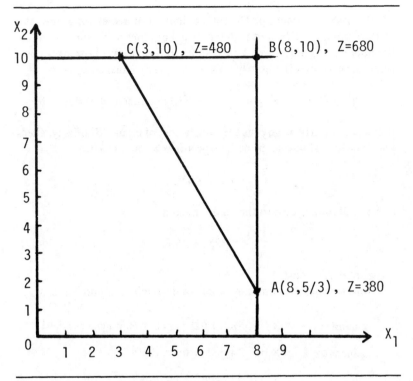

Figure 2.1: Graphical Solution of Example 1

Note that all of the points of Figure 2.1 and inside of the figure satisfy all of the constraints. The minimum value of the objective function occurs at point A, that is, $Z = 380$, $X_1 = 8$, $X_2 = 5/3$. In other words, the company should hire 8 grade 1 inspectors and 1-2/3 grade 2 inspectors to have a total daily cost of $380. This solution satisfies all of the requirements (constraints of the problem). Note that $X_2 = 1$-2/3 could mean, say, hire one full-time grade 2 inspector and a second grade 2 inspector for two-thirds of a day (part-time). Later, a more detailed discussion of the graphical method will be given.

Example 3 (Production planning problem). Three products are processed through three different operations. The time (in minutes) required per unit of each product, the daily capacity of the operation (in minutes/day), and the profit per unit sold of each product (in dollars) are as follows:

	Time per Unit (minutes)			Operation Capacity
Operations	Product 1	Product 2	Product 3	(Minutes/Day)
1	1	2	1	430
2	3	0	2	460
3	1	4	0	420
Profit/Unit	3	2	5	

The zero time indicates that the product does not require the given operation. It is assumed that all units produced are sold. In addition, the given profits per unit are net values after all expenses are deducted. The goal of the model is to determine the optimum daily production that maximizes profit.

SOLUTION

In this example, the model will be stated first. Then answer the questions.

$$\text{maximize } Z = 3X_1 + 2X_2 + 5X_3$$
$$\text{subject to} \quad X_1 + 2X_2 + X_3 \leqslant 430$$
$$3X_1 + \quad 2X_3 \leqslant 460$$
$$X_1 + 4X_2 \quad \leqslant 420$$
$$X_1 \geqslant 0, \; X_2 \geqslant 0, \; X_3 \geqslant 0$$

PROBLEM

(1) What do X_1, X_2, and X_3—that is, the decision variables—represent?

(2) What does the objective function represent?

(3) What are the units of the objective function?

(4) What does each constraint represent?

(5) Are the units on the left- and right-hand sides of the constraints consistent? What are the units for each constraint?

Example 3 will be analyzed in detail in Chapters 4 and 5.

Example 4 (transportation problem). A plastics manufacturer has two plants, one located in Salt Lake City and one in Denver. There are three distribution warehouses, in L.A., Chicago, and New York City. The Salt Lake City plant can supply 120 tons per week and Denver can supply 140 tons per week. The L.A. warehouse needs at least 100 tons each week to meet demands, Chicago needs at least 60 tons weekly, and New York City needs at least 80 tons per week. The following table gives shipping costs (in dollars/ton):

From	L.A.	To Chicago	New York City
Salt Lake City	5	7	9
Denver	6	7	10

How many tons of plastics should be shipped from each plant to each warehouse to minimize the total shipping cost while meeting demands and not exceeding supplies?

SOLUTION

(1) *Decision variables:*

Let X_{11} = number of tons shipped from Salt Lake City to L.A.,

X_{12} = number of tons shipped from Salt Lake City to Chicago,

X_{13} = number of tons shipped from Salt Lake City to New York City,

X_{21} = number of tons shipped from Denver to L.A.,

X_{22} = number of tons shipped from Denver to Chicago, and

X_{23} = number of tons shipped from Denver to New York City.

Observe that by letting $i = 1$ = Salt Lake City, $i = 2$ = Denver, $j = 1$ = L.A., $j = 2$ = Chicago, and $j = 3$ = New York City, then X_{ij}, $i = 1, 2$; $j = 1, 2, 3$, represents the number of tons shipped from *source* i to *destination* j.

(2) *Constraints:*

Supplies:

The *actual* number of tons shipped *from* Salt Lake City is

$$X_{11} + X_{12} + X_{13}$$

and Salt Lake City can only supply up to 120 tons so that

$$X_{11} + X_{12} + X_{13} \leq 120 \text{ (tons per week)}$$

Similarly, the Denver supply constraint is

$$X_{21} + X_{22} + X_{23} \leq 140 \text{ (tons per week)}$$

Demands:

The *actual* number of tons shipped to L.A. is

$$X_{11} + X_{21}$$

and L.A. needs at least 100 tons so that

$$X_{11} + X_{21} \geq 100 \text{ (tons per week)}$$

Similarly, the Chicago demand constraint is

$$X_{12} + X_{22} \geq 60 \text{ (tons per week)}$$

Finally, the New York City demand constraint is

$$X_{13} + X_{23} \geq 80 \text{ (tons per week)}$$

For nonnegativity, $X_{ij} \geq 0$, $i = 1, 2$, $j = 1, 2, 3$.

(3) *Objective function:*

From the shipping cost table, the cost of shipping one ton from Salt Lake City to L.A. is $5, so $5X_{11}$ is the cost of shipping X_{11} tons from Salt Lake City to L.A. The total weekly shipping cost is

$$Z = 5X_{11} + 7X_{12} + 9X_{13} + 6X_{21} + 7X_{22} + 10X_{23} \text{ (in \$ per week)}$$

Thus, the model is

$$\text{minimize} \quad Z = 5X_{11} + 7X_{12} + 9X_{13} + 6X_{21} + 7X_{22} + 10X_{23}$$
(total weekly shipping costs)

subject to
$$X_{11} + X_{12} + X_{13} \leqslant 120 \text{ (SLC supply)}$$
$$X_{21} + X_{22} + X_{23} \leqslant 140 \text{ (Denver supply)}$$
$$X_{11} + X_{21} \geqslant 100 \text{ (L.A. demand)}$$
$$X_{12} + X_{22} \geqslant 60 \text{ (Chicago demand)}$$
$$X_{13} + X_{23} \geqslant 80 \text{ (New York City demand)}$$
$$X_{ij} \geqslant 0, \; i = 1, 2; \; j = 1, 2, 3.$$

Example 4 has two sources and three destinations. For a general transportation problem with m sources, n destinations, unit shipping costs c_{ij}, supplies s_i, and demands d_j the formulation is given by

$$\text{minimize} \quad Z = \sum_{i=1}^{m} \sum_{j=1}^{n} c_{ij} X_{ij}$$

$$\text{subject to} \quad \sum_{j=1}^{n} X_{ij} \leqslant s_i, \quad i = 1, \ldots, m \text{ (supplies)}$$

$$\sum_{i=1}^{m} X_{ij} \geqslant d_j, \quad j = 1, \ldots, n \text{ (demands)}$$

$$X_{ij} \geqslant 0, \; i = 1, \ldots, m; \; j = 1, \ldots, n.$$

Very efficient methods exist for solving transportation problems. The constraints have a special property, called *total unimodularity*, which allows for integer solutions whenever all s_i and d_j are integers. Finally, other models, such as the assignment problem, are closely related to the transportation problem, and can be solved by *network concepts*.

PROBLEM

Answer the same questions as in example 2.

Example 5 (trim-loss problem or paper trim problem or cutting stock problem). A certain paper machine produces paper in a standard width of 180 inches. A set of customer orders for reels of a fixed length (diameter), but varying widths is as follows:

Width (inches)	Number of Reels Ordered
80	200
45	120
27	130

A linear program for cutting the wide reels is required to minimize the total waste at both ends.

SOLUTION

The logical *alternatives* for cutting a 180-inch roll into 80-, 45-, and 27-inch widths are listed in Table 2.1. Note that the logical alternatives are *cutting patterns*, indicating how a *single* 180-inch roll can be cut into the three sizes given. For example, observe that for cutting pattern (alternative) 1, the waste in cutting up a single 180-inch roll is $180 - (2)(80) = 20$ inches. Similarly, verify the waste values for other cutting patterns. It is possible to *generate*, rather than logically determine, cutting patterns for problems of this type and more general problems.

Thus, it is required to minimize the total waste in cutting 180-inch rolls into smaller rolls of the given three sizes while meeting customer demands.

(1) Let X_j = number of 180-inch rolls cut according to pattern j,

$$j = 1, \ldots, 9$$

Then, verify the following model by answering questions as in example 3.

minimize $Z = 20X_1 + 10X_2 + X_3 + 19X_4 + 0X_5 + 18X_6 + 9X_7 + 0X_8 + 18X_9$

subject to
$$2X_1 + X_2 + X_3 + X_4 \geq 200$$
$$2X_2 + X_3 + 4X_5 + 3X_6 + 2X_7 + X_8 \geq 120$$
$$2X_3 + 3X_4 + X_6 + 3X_7 + 5X_8 + 6X_9 \geq 130$$
$$X_j \geq 0, \ j = 1, \ldots, 9.$$

This example could also be modeled using the sum of the Xs as the objective function. The same optimal solution should hold. As X_j represents the number of rolls cut according to the pattern given, only integer solutions make sense. Problems of this kind are *integer* pro-

TABLE 2.1
Alternative j

j	1	2	3	4	5	6	7	8	9
80-inch widths	2	1	1	1	0	0	0	0	0
45-inch widths	0	2	1	0	4	3	2	1	0
27-inch widths	0	0	2	3	0	1	3	5	6
Waste	20	10	1	19	0	18	9	0	18

gramming problems. Although such problems may appear to be simpler to solve than problems with no integer restrictions, quite the opposite is true. Later, we will use the Simplex Method to solve linear programming problems with no integer restrictions. Two solution procedures for solving integer programming problems, called *branch and bound* and *cutting plane* procedures, are ultimately based upon the Simplex procedure. Whereas continuous linear programming problems with hundreds of thousands of variables and tens of thousands of constraints are routinely solved with commercially available computer codes, integer programming problems of hundreds of variables frequently cannot be solved. For this reason, integer programming is a separate field of research with special mathematical modeling and solution procedures that are utilized to exploit integer problems with special structures. Most real-world linear programming problems, unlike integer programming problems, can be solved with current methods. For these reasons, we shall confine our discussion here to linear programming.

The following example, although somewhat more general than the previous example, shows that linear programming techniques provide a procedure for curve-fitting, or regression. Such procedures are frequently superior to the least-squares procedure that is widely accepted in statistics.

Example 6. A scientist has a certain quantity, f, as a function of the variable t. She is interested in determining a mathematical relationship that relates the variables t and f having the form

$$f(t) = at^3 + bt^2 + ct + d$$

from the results of her n experiments (data points) having values $(t_1, f_1), (t_2, f_2), \ldots, (t_n, f_n)$.

The scientist discovers that the values of the unknown coefficients a, b, c, and d must be nonnegative and should add up to one. In order to account for errors (residuals), she defines an error term, e_i, where

$$e_i = f_i - f(t_i), \quad i = 1, \ldots, n$$

She wants to determine the best values for the coefficients a, b, c, and d by using the following criteria (objective functions):

$$Criterion \ 1: \quad \text{minimize } Z = \sum_{i=1}^{n} |e_i|$$

Note: This criterion measures the sum of the absolute deviations.

$$Criterion \ 2: \quad \text{Minimize } Z = \max \{|e_i| : i = 1, \ldots, n\}$$

Note: This criterion measures the maximum absolute deviation. Here, $|e_i|$ is the absolute value of the error associated with the ith data point (experiment).

Remark: In ordinary least-squares regression, the criterion is

$$\text{minimize } Z = \sum_{i=1}^{n} e_i^2$$

which is nonlinear. We will show that both criterion 1 and criterion 2 reduce to linear programming problems.

Observe that

$$e_i = f_i - f(t_i) = f_i - (at_i^3 + bt_i^2 + ct_i + td)$$

For linear programming, it is required that the decision variables be nonnegative, and because e_i is unrestricted in sign, let

$$e_i = e_i^+ - e_i^-,$$

where

$$e_i^+ \geq 0, \quad e_i^- \geq 0, \quad i = 1, \ldots, n$$

where it can be shown that for a given i both of e_i^+ and e_i^- cannot be positive (or, at most one of e_i^+ and e_i^- can be positive). If $e_i^- > 0$, then $e_i^+ = 0$; or, if $e_i^+ > 0$, then $e_i^- = 0$. Thus, if $e_i^- > 0$, then $e_i = -e_i^- < 0$, and if $e_i^+ > 0$, then $e_i = e_i^+ > 0$. Thus, the absolute value of e_i is

$$|e_i| = e_i^+ + e_i^-$$

Then, under criterion 1, we have the following linear programming model:

$$\text{minimize } Z = \sum_{i=1}^{n} (e_i^+ + e_i^-)$$

subject to
$$e_i - (e_i^+ - e_i^-) = 0, \quad i = 1, \dots, n$$

$$e_i - [f_i - (at_i^3 + bt_i^2 + ct_i + d)] = 0, \quad i = 1, \dots, n$$

$$a + b + c + d = 1$$

$$a, b, c, d \geqslant 0, \quad e_i^+, e_i^- \geqslant 0, \quad i = 1, \dots, n.$$

Under criterion 2, the objective function is

$$Z = \max_i \{|e_i| : i = 1, \dots, m\} = \max_i \{e_i^+ + e_i^- : i = 1, \dots, n\}$$

and thus

$$Z \geq e_i^+ + e_i^-, \quad i = 1, \dots, n$$

because Z is the largest of the $e_i^+ + e_i^-$.

Thus, we have the following linear programming model for criterion 2:

$$\text{minimize } Z$$

subject to
$$Z - (e_i^+ + e_i^-) \geqslant 0, \quad i = 1, \dots, n$$

$$e_i - (f_i - (at_i^3 + bt_i^2 + ct_i + d)) = 0, \quad i = 1, \dots, n$$

$$a + b + c + d = 1$$

$$e_i - (e_i^+ - e_i^-) = 0, \quad i = 1, \dots, n$$

$$a, b, c, d \geqslant 0, \quad e_i^+, e_i^- \geqslant 0, \quad i = 1, \dots, n.$$

At least one advantage of these procedures over least squares is that they have less influence from outliers. Furthermore, sensitivity analysis allows for variations in the data points (see Chapter 5).

Example 7. Consider the following *matching problem*, where the variables may be either zero or one (the variables are *binary*). The objective of the Optimal Dating Service is to match as many "compatible" males and females for a Friday evening. Compatibility has been determined from a questionnaire submitted to Optimal Dating Service by each male and female. Consider a 6-male, 5-female problem. In Table 2.2, a number indicates compatibility, whereas a blank indicates no compatibility.

TABLE 2.2

	Ginger	Helen	Jane	Kate	Louise
Arthur				1	
Bob	2	3	4		
Charles				5	
Don			6	7	
Ernest				8	
Fred	9		10		11

Observe that a number only indicates a possible match (not the strength of the match). For example, Ernest-Kate is the eighth possible match.

Let $X_j = 1$ if the jth possible match is made and $X_j = 0$ if the jth match is not made. Then the objective function is

$$\text{maximize } Z = X_1 + X_2 + \ldots + X_{11}$$

As each person can have no more than one date for Friday,

$$X_2 + X_3 + X_4 \leqslant 1 \quad \text{(for Bob)}$$

$$X_6 + X_7 \leqslant 1 \quad \text{(for Don)}$$

$$X_9 + X_{10} + X_{11} \leqslant 1 \quad \text{(for Fred)}$$

$$X_2 + X_9 \leqslant 1 \quad \text{(for Ginger)}$$

$$X_4 + X_6 + X_{10} \leqslant 1 \quad \text{(for Jane)}$$

$$X_1 + X_5 + X_7 + X_8 \leqslant 1 \quad \text{(for Kate)}$$

$$X_j = 0 \text{ or } 1.$$

Notes:

(1) Arthur, Charles, Ernest, Helen, and Louise each have only one possible date, so that they do not need constraints.

(2) Matching problems are different from assignment problems. In assignment problems each person is assigned to one machine and each machine is assigned to one person. In a matching problem, it is possible that a match may not occur (at least one person may not have a date). In fact, in this problem, at least one male will not have a date.

(3) Another possible matching problem occurs in manufacturing assembly, where a manufacturer is assembling shafts and bearings. Due to tolerance specifications, not every shaft will fit into every bearing. It is required to match as many shafts to bearings as possible.

(4) In the dating example, there are 11 binary variables; that is, each variable can be either zero or one. Thus, there are $2^{11} (= 2048)$ possible combinations. Clearly, listing every possibility (*complete enumeration*) is very time consuming. However, *implicit enumeration* procedures such as *Balas's Algorithm*, allow for reductions in the number of possibilities.

Example 8. A political candidate is trying to strictly hold to a budget and determine how many personal appearances as opposed to television appearances he should make in the state presidential primary. The candidate's campaign committee has computed that each personal appearance of a campaign rally costs $15,000, whereas each television speech costs $12,000. He has an efficiency expert who has estimated that each personal appearance rally will yield 30,000 votes, whereas each television appearance will yield 40,000 votes. The candidate knows that he needs at least 240,000 votes in order to win the state. Now, each of his personal appearance trips requires 2 days, whereas a live television run requires just 1 day. He will spend at least 10 days in the state. For each personal appearance the party will provide him with 50 precinct workers but for a television appearance the party can only guarantee 30 precinct workers. The local party boss has announced that the winner must have at least 290 precinct workers. What is the minimum cost at which the candidate can win the state?

Let

X_1 = number of personal appearances, and

X_2 = number of television appearances.

Then the objective is to determine X_1 and X_2 in order to

minimize $Z = 15{,}000X_1 + 12{,}000X_2$ (total campaign cost in dollars)

subject to $\quad 30{,}000X_1 + 40{,}000X_2 \geqslant 240{,}000$ (number of votes to win)

$\qquad\qquad 2X_1 + \quad X_2 \geqslant 10 \quad$ (number of days spent)

$\qquad\qquad 50X_1 + \quad 30X_2 \geqslant 290$ (number of precinct workers)

$\qquad\qquad X_1 \geqslant 0, \quad X_2 = 0$

Notes:

(1) Clearly, only integer solutions make sense here so that this problem is an integer programming problem.

(2) Observe the relative size of the objective function coefficients and the coefficients and right-hand side of the first and third constraints as compared with the coefficients and right-hand side of the second constraint. Problems of this type, where the problem data differ by powers of ten (order of magnitude), are said to be *ill-scaled*. Such problems may not be solvable by a computer code. In order to *rescale* the above problem for solution, divide each term by a positive constant to obtain the following model:

minimize $Z = 5X_1 + 4X_2$

subject to $\quad 3X_1 + 4X_2 \geqslant 24$

$\qquad\qquad 2X_1 + \quad X_2 \geqslant 10$

$\qquad\qquad 5X_1 + 3X_2 \geqslant 29$

$\qquad\qquad X_1, X_2$ nonnegative integers.

Remarks: Another more complicated linear programming political model has been constructed to analyze legislative redistricting. In order to create a linear programming model, it is useful to state the problem as follows:

Suppose that a certain state has m counties where each county i has population $P_i, i = 1, \ldots, m$. Each county is included in a district (a county cannot be divided). The state is assigned K representatives. The problem is to assign each county to a district in such a way that the differences in population among the districts is minimized.

PROBLEM

Try to model the optimal political distribution problem using binary variables (see Garfinkel and Nemhauser, 1970).

3. GRAPHICAL SOLUTION OF LINEAR PROGRAMS IN TWO VARIABLES

After formulating a linear programming problem, we want to solve the problem mathematically to find the best (or optimal) solution. Here, we shall solve a two-variable problem to illustrate the basic concepts used in solving linear programming problems. Several concepts to be discussed in this chapter will provide a basis for understanding the ideas involved in solving general linear programming problems (more than three variables) that follow in subsequent chapters.

Example 1.

$$\text{maximize } Z = 4X_1 + 3X_2$$

$$\text{subject to} \quad 2X_1 + 3X_2 \leqslant 6 \qquad [3.1]$$

$$-3X_1 + 2X_2 \leqslant 3 \qquad [3.2]$$

$$2X_2 \leqslant 5 \qquad [3.3]$$

$$2X_1 + X_2 \leqslant 4 \qquad [3.4]$$

$$X_1 \geqslant 0, X_2 \geqslant 0 \qquad [3.5]$$

The feasible *solution space* is the area enclosed by the constraints 3.1 to 3.5. This region includes both the boundaries and the interior of figure ABCDE. Every point in the solution space satisfies all of the constraints. The optimal solution is the point in the solution space (or *feasible region*) that maximizes Z, the objective function. Note that in example 2 of Chapter 2, the problem was a minimization problem, but this present example is a maximization problem.

Constraints 3.5 specify that solutions must be in the first quadrant, where $X_1 \geq 0$, $X_2 \geq 0$. With constraints 3.1 to 3.5 the resulting solution space is given by the area ABCDE. Note that constraint 3.3 is *redundant*

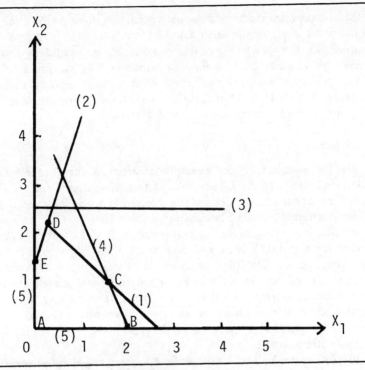

Figure 3.1: Graph of Two-Variable Problem

as it does not affect the solution space (it could be omitted without affecting the solution).

Every point within or on the boundaries of area ABCDE satisfies *all* of the constraints 3.1 to 3.5. Thus, the optimal solution is that (or those) point(s) in ABCDE that gives the maximum value of Z (the objective function value).

For particular values of Z, $4X_1 + 3X_2$ is a family of parallel lines—that is, the parallel lines L_1, L_2, and L_3.

$$L_1: 4X_1 + 3X_2 = 2 \quad (Z = 2)$$
$$L_2: 4X_1 + 3X_2 = 6 \quad (Z = 6)$$
$$L_3: 4X_1 + 3X_2 = 9 \quad (Z = 9)$$

Every point on a parallel line, say on L_1, has the same objective function value. For maximization, such lines are called *isoprofit lines*; for minimization, the lines are termed *isocost lines* as any point on the line has equal profit (cost), or the same objective function value. In general, in mathematical programming (linear or nonlinear programming), such curves are termed *objective function contours*. The maximum of Z occurs at point C because Z has been made as large as possible so that all of the constraints 3.1 to 3.5 are satisfied. To find the coordinates of point C, just find where constraints 3.1 and 3.4 intersect.

Notes:

(1) The solution to this example occurred at the corner point (extreme point) C (3/2, 1). The choice of a specific extreme point as the optimum depends on the slope of the objective function. If we keep the same constraints 3.1 to 3.5 but change the objective function, the solution will still be at one of the extreme points A, B, C, D, and E, but not necessarily at point C. Thus, with constraints 3.1 to 3.5, as the slope of the objective function (the profits per unit) is gradually changed, a critical value of the slope exists, where the optimal solution will change to a different extreme point. In other words, the objective function coefficients (say, unit profits or unit costs) determine which extreme point is the optimal solution as well as the value of the objective function of that extreme point.

(2) For example, if the objective function is changed as follows, the optimum occurs at the indicated point as follows:

Objective Function	Optimum Extreme Point	Optimum Solution
(a) $Z = 10X_1 + X_2$	B	($X_1 = 2$, $X_2 = 0$), $Z = 20$
(b) $Z = X_1 + 20X_2$	D	($X_1 = 3/13$, $X_2 = 24/13$), $Z = 483/18$
(c) $Z = -4X_1 + 2X_2$	E	($X_1 = 0$, $X = 3/2$), $Z = 3$
(d) $Z = -X_1 - X_2$	A	($X_1 = 0$, $X_2 = 0$), $Z = 0$

Verify these graphically.

(3) Thus, the search for an optimal solution is reduced to that of considering only a *finite* number of feasible points; that is, the *extreme points*. Thus, after all of the extreme points are determined, the optimum is the feasible extreme point giving the best (maximum or minimum) value of the objective function.

(4) In our example, there was a single (unique) solution. If, however, the objective function is parallel to the constraint that limits Z, then

there are an infinite number of solutions; that is, if $Z = 2X_1 + 3X_2$, with constraints 3.1 to 3.5, then the solution is $Z = 6$ and includes every value on the line segment joining points D and C. Here, the solution occurred at extreme points D and C (and all other points on the line segment joining D and C). If the optimal solution occurs at two extreme points, then it occurs at every point on the line segment joining the two extreme points.

Example 2. Consider the following problem:

$$\text{maximize } Z = X_1 + 2X_2$$

$$\text{subject to} \quad X_1 + X_2 \geqslant 1 \qquad\qquad [3.1]$$

$$X_2 \leqslant 4 \qquad\qquad [3.2]$$

$$X_1, X_2 \geqslant 0 \qquad\qquad [3.3]$$

Constraint 3.2 restricts X_2 but by 1, $X_1 \geq 1$. Because X_1 is not constrained, Z can get larger and larger. Thus, we have an *unbounded solution.*

PROBLEM

Solve example 2 by the graphical method.

Notes:

(1) It is possible that the constraints have no points in common—there is no point that satisfies all of the constraints. In such cases, there are no extreme points and there is no solution.

(2) In the solution of linear programming problems, the optimal solution may be a single (extreme) point, there may be an infinite number of solutions (joining extreme points), or there may be no solution. This is exactly the situation in solving systems of linear equations, which is what we are doing.

Property: The following property is true for any linear programming problem.

If there is an optimal solution to a linear programming problem, then at least one of the corner points (extreme points) of the feasible region will always qualify to be an optimal solution.

Note: The property gives the fundamental property on which a procedure, called the *Simplex Method*, is based. Also, this means that we need to consider only extreme points, a finite number of points. This property is what makes linear programming so attractive. We never need look for the optimum in the interior or anywhere except the extreme points. The reason for this property is linearity. If any of the constraints or the objective function contains any nonlinear terms, such as X^2 or XY, then this property generally does not hold. Consider a solution space that is a circle and its interior. Clearly, then, we no longer have a finite number of extreme points to examine to determine the optimal solution.

4. THE SIMPLEX METHOD
FOR SOLVING LINEAR PROGRAMS

Standard Form

The Simplex Method requires that the constraints be written as equations and that the problem satisfy additional requirements.

The *standard form* of a general linear programming problem with n variables and m constraints is as follows:

$$\text{maximize } Z = C_1 X_1 + C_2 X_2 + \ldots + C_n X_n$$

$$\text{subject to } \quad a_{11}X_1 + a_{12}X_2 + \ldots + a_{1n}X_{mn} = b_1$$

$$a_{21}X_1 + a_{22}X_2 + \ldots + a_{2n}X_n = b_2$$

$$\vdots \qquad \vdots \qquad\qquad \vdots \qquad \vdots$$

$$a_{m1}X_1 + a_{m2}X_2 + \ldots + a_{mn}X_n = b_m$$

$$X_1, \ldots, X_n \geqslant 0$$

$$b_1, \ldots, b_m \geqslant 0$$

Note: In standard form, note that

(1) the objective function is of maximization type;

(2) the constraints are *equations* (not inequalities);

(3) the decision variables, X_i, are nonnegative;

(4) the right-hand-side constant (resource) of each constraint is non-negative; and

(5) "maximization" of Z can be replaced by "minimization."

Example 1. Consider example 1 of Chapter 2. The linear program is

$$\text{minimize } Z = 40X_1 + 36X_2$$
$$\text{subject to} \quad X_1 \quad \leqslant 8$$
$$X_2 \leqslant 10$$
$$5X_1 + 3X_2 \geqslant 45$$
$$X_1, X_2 \geqslant 0$$

To achieve equality in the first two constraints with nonnegative decision variables, add nonnegative decision variable X_3 to X_1 in the first constraint, and add nonnegative decision variable X_4 to X_2 in the second constraint. The nonnegative variables X_3 and X_4 are called *slack variables*, necessary to achieve an equality from a less-than-or-equal-to constraint. At this point, we have:

$$\text{maximize } Z = 40X_1 + 36X_2 + 0X_3 + 0X_4$$
$$\text{subject to} \quad X_1 \quad + X_3 \quad = 8$$
$$X_2 \quad + X_4 = 10$$
$$5X_1 + 3X_2 \quad \geqslant 45$$
$$X_1, X_2, X_3, X_4 \geqslant 0$$

To achieve standard form, only the last constraint needs to be converted to an equality. This is accomplished by subtracting a nonnegative *surplus variable*, X_5, from the left-hand side of the third constraint (surplus variables achieve equality from greater-than-or-equal-to constraints). Thus, we have:

$$\text{maximize } Z = 40X_1 + 36X_2 + 0X_3 + 0X_4 + 0X_5$$
$$\text{subject to} \quad X_1 \quad + X_3 \quad = 8$$
$$X_2 \quad + X_4 \quad = 10$$

$$5X_1 + 3X_2 \qquad\qquad - X_5 = 45$$
$$X_1, X_2, X_3, X_4, X_5 \geqslant 0$$

Observe that standard form has now been achieved.

Notes:

(1) Occasionally, variables can be positive, negative, or zero; that is, they are unrestricted in sign. If, say, X is unrestricted in sign, then in the model substitute

$$X = X^+ - X^-$$
$$X^+ \geqslant 0, \ X^- \geqslant 0$$

It can be shown that not both X^+ and X^- can be positive. If $X^+ > 0$, then $X^- = 0$ and $X = X^+ > 0$. However, if $X^- > 0$, then $X^+ = 0$ and $X = -X^- < 0$. If both $X^+ = X^+ = 0$, then $X = 0$.

(2) If a constraint of the form ax + by = -5, then to obtain a non-negative right-hand side, multiply both sides by -1 to get -ax - by = 5.

(3) Example 6 of this chapter provides meaning to slack variables.

Solving Systems of Linear Equations and Terminology

In linear programming, we generally are simultaneously solving systems of linear equations with more unknowns (variables) than equations.

Example 2. Consider the following system of two linear equations in five unknowns (n = 5, m = 2):

$$\text{(System 1)} \quad X_1 + 2X_2 + 10X_3 + 4X_4 - 2X_5 = 5 \qquad [4.1]$$

$$X_1 + X_2 + 4X_3 + 3X_4 + X_5 = 8 \qquad [4.2]$$

Because there are more unknowns (n = 5) than equations (m = 2), the system will have more than one solution. In general, the existence of multiple solutions makes the solution of linear programming problems nontrivial.

Definition 1: The set of all possible solutions to a system of linear equations is called the *solution set.*

Definition 2: Two systems of equations are *equivalent* if they have the same solution set.

Note: We can obtain equivalent systems by using two types of *elementary row operations.*

(1) Multiply an equation in the system by a nonzero constant.

(2) Add to any equation a constant multiple of any other equation in the system.

Example 3. An equivalent system to System 1 (S_1), using elementary row operation type 4.2 can be obtained by multiplying equation 4.1 by –1 and adding to 4.2 (subtracting 4.1 from 4.2; that is,

$$(S_2) \quad 1X_1 + 2X_2 + 10X_3 + 4X_4 - 2X_5 = 5 \qquad [4.3]$$

$$0X_1 - 1X_2 + 6X_3 - 1X_4 + 3X_5 = 3 \qquad [4.4]$$

From S_2, we get another equivalent system (S_3) by multiplying 4.4 by 2 and adding to 4.3 (and subsequently multiplying 4.4 by –1).

$$(S_3) \quad 1X_1 + 0X_2 - 2X_3 + 2X_4 + 4X_5 = 11 \qquad [4.5]$$

$$0X_1 + 1X_2 + 6X_3 + 1X_4 - 3X_5 = -3 \qquad [4.6]$$

Notes:

(1) As S_1, S_2, S_3 are equivalent, a solution to one system gives a solution to the other two. Verify this by substituting the solution obtained below in S_1, S_2, and S_3.

(2) In S_3, set $X_3 = X_4 = X_5 = 0$ and solve for X_1 and X_2:

$$X_1 = 11, X_2 = -3, X_3 = 0, X_4 = 0, X_5 = 0$$

or

$$(X_1, X_2, X_3, X_4, X_5) = (11, -3, 0, 0, 0).$$

(3) Systems like S_3 are called *canonical systems*; S_3 has a coefficient of 1 on X_1 in 4.5 and 0 on X_1 in 4.6, whereas X_2 has a coefficient of 0 in 4.5 and 1 in 4.6.

(4) The variables X_1, X_2 are called *basic variables* (X_3, X_4, X_5 are called *nonbasic variables*). By using other elementary row transformations any other two variables could have been made basic variables. Check that there are 10 such pairs—(X_1, X_2), (X_1, X_3), (X_1, X_4), (X_1, X_5), (X_2, X_3), (X_2, X_4), (X_2, X_5), (X_3, X_4), (X_3, X_5), (X_4, X_5). Find all 10 pairs by following example 3.

Definition 3: A variable X_i is said to be a *basic variable* in a given equation if it appears with a coefficient of one in that equation (for X_i) and zeros in all other equations (for X_i). Those variables that are not basic are called *nonbasic variables*.

Definition 4: A *pivot operation* is a sequence of elementary row operations that reduces a given system to an equivalent system where a specified variable has a coefficient of one in one equation and zeros in all of the other equations.

Note: The number of basic variables is equal to the number of equations (constraints) in the system.

Definition 5: The solution obtained from a canonical system by setting the nonbasic variables to zero and solving for the basic variables is called a *basic solution.*

Definition 6: A *basic feasible solution* is a basic solution where values of the basic variables are nonnegative.

Example 4. In example 3, $X_2 = -3$, so the solution $X_1 = 11$, $X_2 = -3$ is basic solution (by definition 5) but not a basic *feasible* solution, by definition 6.

Notes:

(1) For example 3, any two variables out of the five possible could be basic variables; that is, we could have

$$_5C_2 = \binom{5}{2} = \frac{5!}{2!3!} \quad \frac{5 \cdot 4 \cdot 3 \cdot 2 \cdot 1}{(2 \cdot 1)(3 \cdot 2 \cdot 1)} = 10 \text{ basic solutions as listed in note 4.}$$

(2) In general, with n variables and m constraints, the maximum number of basic (not necessarily feasible) solutions is

$$_nC_m = \binom{n}{m} = \frac{n!}{m!\,(n-m)!}$$

(3) The number $_nC_m$ gives an upper bound on the number of feasible extreme points. As shown in example 3, not all such points will be feasible.

(4) If m = n, then

$$_nC_m = \frac{n!}{m!\,(n-m)!} = \frac{n!}{n!\,(n-n)!} = 1 \quad \begin{array}{l}(\text{because } 0! = 1 \\ \text{by definition})\end{array}$$

That is, if the number of variables equals the number of constraints, then there is at most one feasible extreme point. The number $n - m \geq 0$ can be considered to be the number of *degrees of freedom* for optimization. If m = n, then optimization is unnecessary; simply solve the system of equations and evaluate the objective function.

Principles of the Simplex Method

The Simplex Method is an iterative (repetitive) technique for solving linear programming problems expressed in standard form. This technique was developed by George B. Dantzig in 1947. The following scheme provides a basis for the Simplex Method.

General Basic Steps of the Simplex Method

(1) Begin with an initial *basic feasible solution* in canonical form. (*Note:* Step 1 is called an *initialization step*, only used to begin the procedure, and is never returned to.)

(2) Improve the initial solution (from step 1) if possible by finding another basic feasible solution with a better objective function value (larger value if taking the maximum; smaller value if taking the minimum). In this step, the Simplex Method implicitly determines every basic feasible solution that is worse than the current one. This is more efficient than checking all of the extreme points (up to n!/m!(n − m)! possibilities).

(3) Continue (use step 2 to find better basic feasible solutions to improve the objective function). If a particular basic feasible solution cannot be improved, then it is the optimal solution and the Simplex Method terminates. Thus, the Simplex Method moves from an extreme point to an adjacent extreme point in such a way that the objective function never gets worse. The optimal extreme point is obtained when the objective function cannot be further improved by going to an adjacent point.

Example 5. Consider example 3 of Chapter 2 in standard form.

$$\text{maximize } Z = 3X_1 + 2X_2 + 5X_3 + 0X_4 + 0X_5 + 0X_6$$

$$\text{subject to} \quad X_1 + 2X_2 + X_3 + X_4 \qquad\qquad = 430 \quad [4.1]$$

$$3X_1 + \qquad 2X_3 \qquad + X_5 \qquad = 460 \quad [4.2]$$

$$X_1 + 4X_2 \qquad\qquad\qquad + X_6 = 420 \quad [4.3]$$

$$X_1, \ldots, X_6 \geqslant 0,$$

where X_4, X_5, and X_6 are slack variables, used to produce equalities from the less-than-or-equal-to constraints in example 3.

Note: The reader should feel free to graph example 3, Chapter 2 in three dimensions to compare the graphical method with the Simplex Method.

Step 1: Because X_4, X_5, and X_6 appear only in one equation with coefficients of one (with zero coefficients in the other equations), they are the basic variables. We have a canonical system with X_4 X_5, and X_6 as basic variables (and X_1, X_2, and X_3 are nonbasic variables). The corresponding basic solution is $X_1 = X_2 = X_3 = 0$, (because X_1, X_2, and X_3 are nonbasic variables), and thus $X_4 = 430$, $X_5 = 460$, $X_6 = 420$, with objective function value $Z = 3 \cdot 0 + 2 \cdot 0 + 5 \cdot 0 + 0 \cdot 430 + 0 \cdot 460 + 0 \cdot 420 = 0$. In this example, recall that the objective function represents total daily profit. At this point in the procedure, the total profit is \$0, where $X_1 = X_2 = X_3 = 0$; that is, produce zero units of products 1, 2, and 3. At this point, we seek to improve (increase) the objective function value (total daily profits). To do this, the Simplex Method checks to see if a *better* basic feasible solution can be found, for which Z is larger.

Definition: An *adjacent basic feasible solution* differs from the present basic feasible solution in exactly one variable.

If the basic feasible solution is not optimal, then the Simplex Method obtains an adjacent basic feasible solution with a value of Z not less than the present value of Z for maximization. To do this, one of the nonbasic variables is made basic. The exchange is done in such a way as to give maximum improvement to the value of the objective function. Because in any basic feasible solution the basic variables are positive whereas nonbasic variables are zero, making a nonbasic variable a basic variable is the same as increasing its value to a positive quantity, where the choice of *which* nonbasic variable to use is the one that can improve Z the most. This is decided by increasing the value of the nonbasic variable by one unit and checking the resulting change in the value of the objective function. This is done for each of the existing nonbasic variables, one at a time.

Consider the nonbasic variable X_3; increase X_3 from 0 to 1 and check its effect on the objective function (Z increases by 5 for a unit increase in X_3). We are checking adjacent feasible solutions, so X_1 and X_2 will remain zero. Thus, because $X_1 = X_2 = 0$, constraints 4.1, 4.2, and 4.3 become

$$X_3 + X_4 \qquad\qquad = 430 \qquad\qquad [4.4]$$

$$2X_3 \qquad + X_5 \quad = 460 \qquad\qquad [4.5]$$

$$X_6 = 420 \qquad\qquad [4.6]$$

$$X_3, X_4, X_5, X_6 \geqslant 0$$

Thus, the *net change in Z per unit increase in* $X_3 = Z_{new} - Z_{old} = 5 - 0 = 5$, and this is called the *relative profit* of the nonbasic variable X_3. Verify that the relative (net or marginal) profit of X_1 is 3 and X_3 is 2, and this is why X_3 was chosen to become a basic variable; that is, X_3 is the *entering variable* (X_3 entered the basis).

The decision to make X_3 the entering variable was based on a unit increase in X_3 to increase Z by 5. At this point, it is of interest to determine the largest value that X_3 can take on without making any of the variables X_4, X_5, or X_6 negative. Because a unit increase in X_3 increases Z by 5 units, the new objective function value will be five times the largest value of X_3.

Now, by constraint 4.4, if $X_3 = 430 = 430/1$, then $X_4 = 0$; by constraint 4.5, if $X_3 = 230 = 460/2$, then $X_5 = 0$; and by constraint 4.6 no values of X_3 (420/0 does not exist) can make $X_6 = 0$. To ensure that no variables become negative, the largest value of X_3 is $X_3 = 230$, so that $X_5 = 0$; that is, the maximum increase in $X_3 = \min \{430/1, 460/2, 420/0\} = \min \{420,$

$230, \underline{\quad} \} = 230$ [if $X_3 = 430$, then, by constraint 4.5 $X_5 = 460 - 2 \cdot (430) = -200 < 0$ is infeasible; if $X_3 = 230$, then $X_4 = 200$ by constraint 4.4 and $X_5 = 0$; X_5 becomes a nonbasic variable]. The new nonbasic variable X_5 is called the *leaving variable* (X_5 left the basis).

Because a unit increase in X_3 increases Z by 5 units and X_3 can be increased to a maximum of 230, the net increase in the objective function is $5(230) = 1150$; by increasing to 230 the number of units of product 3 increases profits by $1150. As pointed out, when X_3 is increased to 230, the basic variable X_5 decreases to 0 (and thus becomes nonbasic). Thus, the new basic feasible solution is $X_1 = X_2 = 0$, $X_5 = 0$, $X_3 = 230$, $X_4 = 200$, $X_6 = 420$ and $Z = 1150$. We have thus increased daily profits from $0 to $1150 by entering X_3 (producing 230 units of product 3) and forcing X_5 to zero.

Equivalently, we can do these steps by performing a pivot operation on X_3 as follows:

(1) Divide constraint 4.2 by 2 to reduce the coefficient of X_3 to 1.

(2) Multiply constraint 4.2 by $-1/2$ and add to constraint 4.1 to eliminate X_3 in constraint 4.1.

(3) Do nothing to constraint 4.3.

$$-1/2X_1 + 2X_2 + 0X_3 + 1X_4 - 1/2X_5 + 0X_6 = 200 \qquad [4.7]$$

$$3/2X_1 + 0X_2 + 1X_3 + 0X_4 + 1/2X_5 + 0X_6 = 230 \qquad [4.8]$$

$$X_1 + 4X_2 + 0X_3 + 0X_4 + 0X_5 + 1X_6 = 420 \qquad [4.9]$$

$$X_1, \ldots, X_6 \geqslant 0$$

Note that the coefficients of the variables X_3, X_4 and X_6 in constraints 4.7, 4.8, and 4.9 consist of zeros and a single one. This means that X_3, X_4, and X_6 are basic variables and thus, X_1, X_2, and X_5 are nonbasic variables (equal to zero). Clearly, $X_4 = 200$ (by constraint 4.7), $X_3 = 230$ (by constraint 4.8), and $X_6 = 420$ (by constraint 4.9), the same as above.

Again, the Simplex Method checks to see if this basic feasible solution is optimal by computing relative profits for all nonbasic variables. If any relative profit is positive, then a new basic feasible solution with improved Z is obtained as before. This process continues until all relative profits of all nonbasic variables are nonpositive (negative or zero), so that the basic feasible solution cannot be further improved—that is, we have optimality. If possible, continue as above. The above discussion is instructive, but such a procedure is not computationally efficient. The subsequent discussion will result in a more efficient, equivalent procedure to that shown above.

Condition for Optimality

For *maximization* (minimization), a basic feasible solution is *optimal* if the relative (marginal or net) profits of the nonbasic variables are all nonpositive (nonnegative).

Summary of the Simplex Method
(Basic Steps for a Maximization Problem)

(1) *Initialization.* Start with an initial basic feasible solution in canonical form.

(2) *Optimality.* Check for optimality. Here, the relative profits of all nonbasic variables are computed. If the relative profits are nonpositive, STOP—the solution is optimal. Otherwise, go to step 3.

(3) *Entering variable.* Choose a nonbasic variable to be the new basic variable, where a general rule is to choose the nonbasic variable with the largest (positive) relative profit in order to give a large increase in Z.

(4) *Leaving variable.* Determine the (old) basic variable to be replaced by the (new) basic variable. Examine each constraint to see how far the new basic variable can be increased. Examine the coefficients of the new basic variable in each of the constraints. If a constraint has a *positive* coefficient, then the maximum increase *for that constraint* is the right-hand side constant (resource) divided by the positive coefficient. (If a constraint has a nonpositive coefficient, then the maximum increase in the new basic variable for that constraint is infinite. If the coefficients of the entering variable in *all* constraints are nonpositive, then the entering variable can be increased indefinitely, and thus the solution is unbounded.) To satisfy *all* of the constraints (for feasibility), take the minimum of these ratios. This rule usually is called the *minimum ratio rule.*

(5) *Pivot.* Find the new canonical system and the *basic feasible solution* by a pivot operation. Go to step 2.

The following flowchart describes the Simplex Method (Figure 4.1).

42

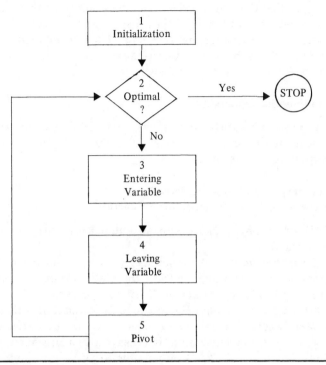

Figure 4.1: The Simplex Model

The Simplex Method in Tableau Form

The steps of the Simplex Method can be used more efficiently by creating a tableau to represent the objective function and the constraints. Also, by some simple formulas, the computations can be made mechanical.

Example 6. Consider example 5. This can be expressed by Tableau 4.1.

TABLEAU 4.1

C_B	C_j Basis	3 X_1	2 X_2	5 X_3	0 X_4	0 X_5	0 X_6	Constants
0	X_4	1	2	1	1	0	0	430
0	X_5	3	0	2	0	1	0	460
0	X_6	1	4	0	0	0	1	420

Basic refers to the basic variables in the current basic feasible solution; that is, X_4 X_5, and X_6 are the basic variables. If a variable is not in the basis, it is a nonbasic variable and is equal to zero: $X_1 = X_2 = X_3 = 0$. The *values* of basic variables are in the column "constants" ($X_4 = 430$, $X_5 = 460$, $X_6 = 420$; $X_1 = X_2 = X_3 = 0$). Also, the column C_B gives the objective function coefficients of the basic variables. The value of the objective function is $Z = 3 \cdot 0 + 2 \cdot 0 + 5 \cdot 0 + 0 \cdot 430 + 0 \cdot 460 + 0 \cdot 420 = 0$. (Compare with example 5.) Observe that at this point, the original problem, without slack variables—variables X_1, X_2, and X_3—is zero; the initial basic feasible solution is at the origin in $X_1 - X_2 - X_3$ space (in 3-space).

To check for optimality, we need the relative profits of all nonbasic variables, which can be computed by a formula called the *inner product rule*; that is, relative profit of $X_j = \overline{C_j} = C_j -$ [sum of products of elements in C_B and (times, or multiplied by) the column elements under X_j] $= C_j - Z_j$, where C_j is the objective function coefficient (unit profit) of variable X_j.

Thus,

$$\overline{C_1} = 3 - (0 \cdot 1 + 0 \cdot 3 + 0 \cdot 1) = 3$$
$$\overline{C_2} = 2 - (0 \cdot 2 + 0 \cdot 0 + 0 \cdot 4) = 2$$
$$\overline{C_3} = 5 - (0 \cdot 1 + 0 \cdot 2 + 0 \cdot 0) = 5$$

PROBLEM

Calculate $\overline{C_4}$, $\overline{C_5}$, and $\overline{C_6}$. (You should get zero for each. Explain why.) To answer the question, the relative profit, $\overline{C_j} = C_j - Z_j$, gives the increase in the objective function for a unit increase in a current nonbasic variable. Because X_4, X_5, and X_6 are already basic variables, they cannot improve the value of the objective function by making them basic variables because they already are basic variables.

Note: In the rule for computing the relative profits, the (sum of the products of C_B elements times the column elements under X_j) are denoted by Z_j; that is, $\overline{C_j} = C_j - Z_j$.

Because C_j is unit profits, Z_j is "imputed costs." Thus, $\overline{C_j} = C_j - Z_j$ represents net (marginal or relative) profits—that is, profits minus costs, or the increase in the objective function value when current nonbasic variable X_j is increased from zero to one (unit increase).

PROBLEM

Give an economic interpretation of the Simplex Method. For maximization (minimization) problems continue as long as at least one $\overline{C_j}$ is positive (negative); that is, as long as the objective function keeps getting larger (smaller).

Tableau 4.2 can be constructed by putting the relative profit row onto Tableau 4.1.

TABLEAU 4.2

C_B	C_j Basis	3 X_1	2 X_2	5 X_3	0 X_4	0 X_5	0 X_6	Constants
0	X_4	1	2	1	1	0	0	430
0	X_5	3	0	(2)	0	1	0	460
0	X_6	1	4	0	0	0	1	420
	Z_j	0	0	0	0	0	0	
$\overline{C}_j = C_j - Z_j$		3	2	5	0	0	0	

Because there are three positive values in the $\overline{C}$ row, the current basic feasible solution is not optimal. The nonbasic variable X_3 gives the largest per-unit increase in Z ($\overline{C}_3 = 5$ is the largest positive relative profit), so X_3 is chosen as the *entering variable*. (The column circled under X_3 is called the *pivot column*).

To decide the *leaving variable*, use the minimum ratio rule (form ratios of constants divided by corresponding pivot column elements).

	Row	Basic Variable	Upper Limit on X_3
	1	X_4	$430/1 = 430$
pivot row →	2	X_5 leaving variable	$460/2 = 230$ minimum ratio
	3	X_6	$420/0$

The circled row in Tableau 4.2, corresponding to the leaving variable, X_5, is called the *pivot row*. The circled element (2) is called the *pivot element*. The pivot element is the intersection of the pivot column and the pivot row. (The first step of the pivot operation is to divide every number in the pivot row by the pivot element to produce a one in the next tableau in the pivot element cell, and the new right-hand side is the minimum ratio.)

Thus, X_5 is the leaving variable and X_3 is the entering variable, so the new basis contains X_4, X_3, and X_6 as basic variables, as in example 5. The *new* canonical system is obtained by performing a pivot operation as follows:

(1) Divide pivot row (row 2) by the pivot element, 2, to produce a coefficient of 1 for X_3 in the pivot row (and the right-hand side becomes the minimum ratio, $460/2 = 230$).

(2) Eliminate X_3 from row 1 by multiplying row 2 by $-1/2$ and adding to row 1. (As row 3 already has a coefficient of 0 for X_3, do nothing in row 3.)

For the entering variable, the pivot operation will produce constraint coefficients of zero in all rows except for the pivot row, where the coefficient is one. After the pivot operation, the new constraint coefficients of the entering variable indicate that it is now a basic variable (see Tableau 4.3).

TABLEAU 4.3

	C_j	3	2	5	0	0	0		
C_B	Basis	X_1	X_2	X_3	X_4	X_5	X_6	Constants	Ratios
0	X_4	$-1/2$	2	0	1	$-1/2$	0	200	$200/2 = 100$
5	X_3	$3/2$	0	1	0	$1/2$	0	230	$230/0$
0	X_6	1	4	0	0	0	1	420	$420/4 = 105$
	z_j	$15/2$	0	5	0	$5/2$	0		
$\bar{C}$ row		$-9/2$	2	0	0	$-5/2$	0	$Z = 1{,}150$	

Compare this solution with example 5.

The current basic feasible solution is $Z = 0 \cdot 200 + 5 \cdot 230 + 0 \cdot 420 = 1150$, and the relative profits for the nonbasic variables

$$\bar{C}_1 = C_1 - Z_1 = 3 - (0 \cdot (-1/2) + 5 \cdot 3/2 + 0 \cdot 1) = -9/2$$

$$\bar{C}_2 = C_2 - Z_2 = 2 - (0 \cdot 2 + 5 \cdot 0 + 0 \cdot 4) \qquad = 2$$

$$\bar{C}_5 = C_5 - Z_5 = 0 - (0 (-1/2) + 5 \cdot 1/2 + 0 \cdot 0) = -5/2$$

Because $C_2 - Z_2 = 2$, which is positive, the entering variable is X_2, and by the minimum ratio rule X_4 *leaves* the basis.

Divide the pivot row by 2 (the pivot element) and get zero coefficients for X_2 in row 2 (check the following tableau):

TABLEAU 4.4

	C_j	3	2	5	0	0	0	
C	Basis	X_1	X_2	X_3	X_4	X_5	X_6	Constants
2	X_2	−1/4	1	0	1/2	−1/4	0	100
5	X_3	3/2	0	1	0	1/2	0	230
0	X_6	2	0	0	−2	1	1	20
$C_j − Z_j$ row		−4	0	0	−1	−2	0	Z = 1,350

Verify the elements in Tableau 4.4. Note that the solution is optimal. What tells you this? (The relative profits are nonpositive.) Give the solution and interpret the problem. ($X_1 = 0$, $X_2 = 100$, $X_3 = 230$; that is, produce no units of product 1, 100 units of product 2, and 230 units of product 3 to obtain a total daily profit of $1350.) Note that $X_6 = 20$. What does this say? That the slack variable is positive means that the third constraint is *loose*; although the solution is optimal, 20 minutes of operation 3's time was not used in producing products, 1, 2, and 3. However, as $X_4 = X_5 = 0$, constraints 1 and 2 are *tight*, that is, satisfied as equations, and thus all of the time allocated in operations 1 and 2 was used up. Thus, the optimal solution need not consume all of the resources. Furthermore, note that although the unit profit of product 1 is $3 is larger than the unit profit of product 2 ($2), it is optimal to produce 100 units of product 2 and no units of product 1. In Chapter 5, we will determine how large the unit profit on product 1 (objective function coefficient of X_1) has to be to make it profitable to produce product 1 (for X_1 to enter the basis).

Finding a Feasible Basis

The Simplex Method needs an initial basic feasible solution in canonical form, but his may not be readily available for some linear programming problems. (This situation did not arise in examples 5 and 6.) If we have such a situation, there are two basic approaches that are used.

(A) *Trial and Error:* Here, a basic variable is chosen *arbitrarily* for each constraint and the system is reduced to canonical form. If it is a basic *feasible* solution, then the simplex method may begin. Otherwise, choose another combination of variables. Clearly, this is inefficient, as shown by example 3 of Chapter 4, choosing X_1 and X_2.

(B) *Use of Artificial Variables:* When a canonical system with a basic feasible solution is not available by inspection (looking at the problem), the following procedure provides a systematic way of achieving one:

   (a) The linear programming problem is converted to *standard form.*

   (b) Each constraint is checked to find a basic variable.

   (c) If no basic variable is found in a constraint(s), then a new (artificial) basic variable is added to *serve* as a basic variable, so that each constraint has a basic variable (we then have a canonical system).

Notes:

(1) The new (artificial) variables have *no meaning* in the original problem. Their only purpose is to provide a canonical system to *begin* the Simplex Method and they will eventually be forced to zero (unless the *original* problem has no solution). In other words, if artificial variables are basic variables (positive) in the optimal solution, then this means that the solution is "artificial"; that is, there is no solution.

(2) There are two basic artificial variables methods: (a) the Big M method, and (b) the two-phase method. In the two-phase approach, the first phase consists of minimizing the sum of the artificial variables (objective function) subject to the original constraints with artificial variables. Once the objective function value equals zero (meaning that all artificial variables equal zero because of nonnegativity), the artificial variables are eliminated from the tableau and the first tableau in Phase II is formed from the last tableau in Phase I (minus the artificial variables). In this monograph, however, we will study the Big M approach.

**The Big M Simplex Method
(or Method of Penalty)**

In this approach, each of the artificial variables is assigned a very large coefficient (penalty) in the objective function. The Simplex Method will subsequently force the artificial variables to zero as they will be uneconomical to maintain as basic variables—they will be replaced by basic variables with small costs.

Note: In particular, assume that M is a *very* large positive number. Assign +M as the coefficients of the artificial variables in a *minimization* problem (and −M as the coefficients of the artificial variables in a *maximization* problem). As we will see in the following example, the artificial variables are found in the initial basic feasible solution (initial tableau), and the assignment of a large objective function coefficient is deliberately made to ensure that the Simplex Method will cause them to leave the basis (become zero) and only the original variables in standard form remain as basic variables.

Example 7.

$$\text{minimize } Z = 4X_1 + X_2$$

$$\text{subject to} \quad X_1 + 2X_2 \leqslant 3$$

$$3X_1 + X_2 = 3$$

$$4X_1 + 3X_2 \geqslant 6$$

$$X_1, X_2 \geqslant 0$$

PROBLEM

Solve this problem graphically. In this example, there is a less-than-or-equal to constraint, an equality constraint, and a greater-than-or-equal to constraint. The latter two constraints require artificial variables when solving by the simplex algorithm.

(a) First, convert to standard form

$$\text{minimize } Z = 4X_1 + X_2 + 0X_3 + 0X_4$$

$$\text{subject to} \quad X_1 + 2X_2 + X_3 \qquad = 3 \qquad [4.1]$$

$$3X_1 + X_2 \qquad = 3 \qquad [4.2]$$

$$4X_1 + 3X_2 \qquad - X_4 = 6 \qquad [4.3]$$

$$X_1, X_2, X_3, X_4 \geqslant 0$$

(b) Constraints 4.2 and 4.3 do *not* give obvious basic feasible variables, but X_3 can be used as a starting basic variable for constraint 4.1.

(c) Adding artificial variables X_5 and X_6 to constraints 4.2 and 4.3 *and* MX_5 and MX_6 to the objective function, we get minimize $Z = 4X_1 + 1X_2 + 0X_3 + 0X_4 + MX_5 + MX_6$

subject to $\quad 1X_1 + 2X_2 + 1X_3 + 0X_4 + 0X_5 + 0X_6 = 3$

$\quad\quad\quad 3X_1 + 1X_2 + 0X_3 + 0X_4 + 1X_5 + 0X_6 = 3$

$\quad\quad\quad 4X_1 + 3X_2 + 0X_3 + (-1)X_4 + 0X_5 + 1X_6 = 6$

$\quad\quad\quad X_1, \ldots, X_6 \geqslant 0$

The initial Simplex tableau is as follows in Tableau 4.5 (with X_3, X_5, and X_6 as basic variables):

TABLEAU 4.5

C_B	C_j Basis	4 X_1	1 X_2	0 X_3	0 X_4	M X_5	M X_6	Constants
0	X_3	1	2	1	0	0	0	3
M	X_5	3	1	0	0	1	0	3
M	X_6	4	3	0	−1	0	1	6
	$\overline{C}_j$	4-7M	1-4M	0	M	0	0	Z = 9M

Verify that the entries are correct. If M = 1 million, then the objective function value is Z = 9 million, and we are minimizing. Thus, there is a severe penalty for having artificial variables X_5 and X_6 in the basis.

For *minimization* problems the *most negative* $\overline{C}_j = C_j - Z_j$ (relative *cost* or optimality indicator) gives the entering variable. Thus, X_1 is the *entering* variable (and the column below X_1 is the pivot column).

For the *leaving* variable, divide the elements under constants by the corresponding elements in the pivot column and take the minimum of these ratios, that is,

$$\min \{3/1, \; 3/3, \; 6/4\} = 3/3 = 1, \text{ corresponding to } X_5$$
$$X_3 \quad X_5 \quad X_6$$

Artificial variable X_5 leaves (and the pivot is row 2). Also, 3 is the pivot element.

Check the following tableau (Tableau 4.6):

TABLEAU 4.6

C_B	Basis	C_j 4 X_1	1 X_2	0 X_3	0 X_4	M X_5	M X_6	Constants
0	X_3	0	5/3	1	0	−1/3	0	2
4	X_1	1	1/3	0	0	1/3	0	1
M	X_6	0	5/3	0	−0	−4/3	1	2
$\overline{C}$ row		0	(−1/3−5/3M)	0	M	(7/3M−4/3)	0	Z = 4+2M

Note that Z has decreased from Tableau 4.1 to Tableau 4.3 from 9M to 4 + 2M. Clearly, X_2 enters. There is a tie in the minimum ratio rule between X_3 and X_6, which is usually broken arbitrarily. As X_6 is an artificial variable, choose X_6 as the leaving variable.

PROBLEM 1

Do *two more* iterations (tableaus) to get an optimal solution of $X_1 = 3/5$, $X_2 = 6/5$, $Z = 18/5$. Verify by your graphical solution to the original two-variable problem.

PROBLEM 2

Solve example 1 of Chapter 2 by the Big M method (and check by example 2, Chapter 2).

5. SENSITIVITY (OR POSTOPTIMALITY) ANALYSIS

Following formulation and solution of a linear programming problem, it frequently is important to consider variations in the coefficients of the variables in the objective function and/or constraints, and/or resources (right-hand sides). This kind of analysis is known as *sensitivity analysis* or *postoptimality analysis*. We will consider (1) changes in the objective function coefficients (corresponding to current *basic* and *non-basic* variables), and (2) changes in the resources (right-hand sides). Also, we will change just one coefficient (or resource) at a time (we will *not* consider simultaneous changes). *Parametric programming* allows for the analysis of simultaneous changes of these elements as well as constraint (*technological*) coefficients. It is also possible to consider the affect of adding constraint(s) and/or variable(s) subsequent to solving the original problem.

Example 1. Consider example 6 of Chapter 4 (production planning problem).

$$\text{maximize } Z = 3X_1 + 2X_2 + 5X_3 + 0X_4 + 0X_5 + 0X_6$$

$$
\begin{aligned}
\text{subject to} \quad & X_1 + 2X_2 + X_3 + X_4 && = 430 \quad \text{(operation 1)} \\
& 3X_1 + 2X_3 + X_5 && = 460 \quad \text{(operation 2)} \\
& X_1 + 4X_2 && + X_6 = 420 \quad \text{(operation 3)} \\
& X_1, \ldots, X_6 \geqslant 0
\end{aligned}
$$

where X_1, X_2, and X_3 are the numbers of products 1, 2, and 3 to produce and X_4, X_5, and X_6 are slack variables (times in minutes) corresponding to operations 1, 2, and 3, respectively.

Tableau 5.1 is the optimal tableau from example 6 of Chapter 4 is:

TABLEAU 5.1

	C_j	3	2	5	0	0	0	
C_B	Basis	X_1	X_2	X_3	X_4	X_5	X_6	Constants
2	X_2	$-1/4$	1	0	1/2	$-1/4$	0	100
5	X_3	3/2	0	1	0	1/2	0	230
0	X_6	2	0	0	-2	1	1	20
$C_j - Z_j$		-4	0	0	-1	-2	0	$Z = 1,350$

Changes in the Objective Coefficients (Objective Function Coefficient Ranging)

CHANGES IN THE NONBASIC COEFFICIENTS

Assume that the objective function coefficient for *nonbasic* variable X_1 was not known with certainty (or management may want to change the net profit per unit of product 1). The current solution (basis) will remain optimal as long as the marginal profit $\overline{C}_1 \leq 0$, and this condition causes X_1 to remain a nonbasic variable ($X_1 = 0$). As it is of interest to change this coefficient, denote it as C_1. Now, by definition,

$$\overline{C}_1 = C_1 - Z_1 = C_1 - 7 \leq 0,$$

that is,

$$C_1 \leq 7$$

This means that X_1 remains a nonbasic variable ($X_1 = 0$, that is, do not produce product 1 as long as $C_1 \leq 7$, or the net profit per unit of product 1 is seven dollars or less). By substitution, when $C_1 = 7$, then $\overline{C}_1 = 0$ (if $\overline{C}_j = 0$ when X_j is nonbasic, then this means that there is an alternate optimal solution), that is, $C_1 = 7$ is the value where X_1 can enter the basis. If $C_1 > 7$, then $\overline{C}_1 > 0$ and X_1 becomes a basic variable. In other words, by varying C_1 only, the current optimal basis consisting of X_2, X_3, and X_6 remains as long as

$$-\infty < C_1 \leq 7$$

and within this range, varying C_1 does not affect the value of the objective function because $X_1 = 0$.

In other words, management must make the unit profit on product 1 at least 7 dollars in order to realize a profit from producing product 1. If $C_1 > 7$, then X_1 enters the basis and verify that X_6 is the leaving variable. Frequently, only one more iteration will be required to restore optimality (set $C_1 = 8$ and obtain the new optimal solution). Thus, C_1 can be increased from 3 to 7 ($7 - 3 = 4$) and the solution will stay optimal. Note also that current $\overline{C}_1 = -4$ so that C_1 can be increased by 4 to 7 (from 3).

PROBLEM

For the other nonbasic variables, X_4 and X_5, check that C_4 can be increased by 1 and C_5 can be increased by $-(-2) = 2$.

Note. If these coefficients are increased beyond these ranges, then the corresponding relative profit $\overline{C}$ will become positive. Then that variable will enter and it will be necessary to find the leaving variable. Also, within the range, varying the objective function coefficient does not affect either the value of the objective function or the status of any other variables.

CHANGES IN THE COEFFICIENTS OF BASIC VARIABLES

Consider the coefficient of the *basic* variable X_2. Let us find a range for C_2 (the unknown coefficient of X_2). Then the current solution (X_2, X_3, and X_6 basic variables with all $\overline{C}_j$ nonpositive) will be optimal as long as the $\overline{C}$ values (marginal profits) are nonpositive for all nonbasic variables (inasmuch as relative profits $\overline{C}$ are zero for basic variables) $\overline{C}_1 \leq 0$, $\overline{C}_4 \leq 0$, and $\overline{C}_5 \leq 0$. Observe that a change in a coefficient of a *nonbasic* variable only affects the marginal profit for that nonbasic variable, but a change in a coefficient of a *basic* variable generally affects the marginal profits of *all* nonbasic variables. Now, by the above conditions,

$$\overline{C}_1 = 3 - (-1/4C_2 + 15/2 + 0) = 1/4C_2 - 9/2 \leq 0$$

or

$$C_2 \leq 18 \qquad\qquad [5.1]$$

Satisfying condition 5.1 results in $C_1 \leq 0$, (keeps X_1 nonbasic), so that, if $C_2 > 18$, then X_1 enters the basis. Now,

$$\overline{C}_4 = 0 - (1/2C_2 + 0 + 0) = -1/2C_2 \leq 0$$

or

$$C_2 \geq 0 \qquad\qquad [5.2]$$

Satisfaction of condition 5.2 ensures that $\overline{C}_4 \leq 0$ (keeps X_4 nonbasic), so that, if $C_2 < 0$, then X_4 enters the basis. Now, finally,

$$\overline{C}_5 = 0 - (-1/4C_2 + 5/2 + 0) = 1/4C_2 - 5/2 \leq 0$$

or

$$C_2 \leq 10 \qquad\qquad [5.3]$$

Satisfaction of condition 5.3 ensures that $C_5 \leq 0$ (X_5 is kept nonbasic), so that, if $C_2 > 10$, the X_5 will become a basic variable. If $10 < C_2 \leq 18$, then by conditions 5.1 and 5.3 X_1 will remain nonbasic but X_5 will enter the basis. In order to retain X_2, X_3, and X_6 as basic variables (X_1, X_4, and X_5 as nonbasic variables), all three of the conditions 5.1, 5.2, and 5.3 must be satisfied simultaneously. Verify that this gives

$$0 \leq C_2 \leq 10 \qquad\qquad [5.4]$$

PROBLEM

Range the objective function coefficient of the basic variable X_3. *Note:* Observe that, within the range of variation, changes in the objective function coefficient of a basic variable cause the value of the objective function to change (unlike the case for nonbasic variables). For example, for the range obtained in condition 5.4 observe that the objective function varies as

54

$$1150 \le Z \le 2150$$

when

$$0 \le C_2 \le 10$$

and $Z = 1350$ when $C_2 = 2$, as in the final tableau.

PROBLEM

For the range obtained for C_3 in the previous problem, determine the corresponding variation in the objective function. *Note:* Economically, the above analysis for C_2 means that, if the unit profit for product 2 is varied from \$0 to \$10, the total daily profit varies from \$1150/day to \$2150/day by producing 100 units of product 2, 230 units of product 3 (and 0 units of product 1), and 20 minutes of slack time for operation 3.

Changes in the Resources
(Right-Hand-Side Constants)

Suppose that either the resources were not originally known with certainty or one or more resources may be changed by management. In the product planning problem, this may mean that, say, the operation capacity (in minutes/day) may change from 430 to 431 or to 423, or, in general to $430 + \Delta b_1$, where Δb_1 may be either positive or negative (or zero).

Note: Δb_1 is the change in resource 1 from its original value. (Δb_2 and Δb_3 are the respective changes in resources 2 and 3 from original resource values.)

The original problem with a change in the operation 1 capacity may then be written as

$$
\begin{aligned}
\text{maximize } Z = 3X_1 &+ 2X_2 + 5X_3 + 0X_4 + 0X_5 + 0X_6 \\
\text{subject to} \quad X_1 &+ 2X_2 + X_3 + X_4 && = 430 + \Delta b_1 \\
3X_1 & + 2X_3 + X_5 && = 460 \\
X_1 &+ 4X_2 && + X_6 = 420 \\
X_1, &\ldots, X_6 \ge 0
\end{aligned}
$$

This problem could be solved to obtain an optimal solution (try this if you are unconvinced). If it is, the following *general principle* is obtained.

If some amount, Δb_i, is added to the right-hand side of the ith constraint in a linear programming problem (*original* problem), then the components of the right-hand side of the optimal solution will be given by the right-hand side constant plus Δb_i times the corresponding coefficient of the ith slack (or artificial) variable in the optimal solution.

Note: Put another way, when a resource availability is uncertain, then one of the constraints is being examined; in our case, it is the first (operation 1) constraint. *Prior* to solving by the simplex method (in the initial tableau), a slack variable (X_4 = 430, or possibly an artificial variable in general) was part of the initial basic feasible solution and X_4 corresponds to the first constraint. Now, the principle says that the elements of this column (under X_4) in the optimal tableau in the constraint are used to express the optimal solution to the problem in terms of Δb_1.

The example below illustrates the general principle.

Example 1. Recall that the optimal solution from example 6 of Chapter 4 is seen in Tableau 4.4:

TABLEAU 4.4

C	C_j Basis	3 X_1	2 X_2	5 X_3	0 X_4	0 X_5	0 X_6	Constants
2	X_2	−1/4	1	0	1/2	−1/4	0	100
5	X_3	3/2	0	1	0	1/2	0	230
0	X_6	2	0	0	−2	1	1	20
	$C_j − Z_j$ row	−4	0	0	−1	−2	0	Z = 1,350

The column under X_4 was originally associated with the first constraint. (X_4 was associated with the first constraint in the initial basic feasible solution, and, in fact, X_4 was the basic variable from the first constraint in the initial tableau.)

Now, from the principle, the optimal solution (with a change, Δb_1, in the first resource) is written as follows:

$$\hat{X}_2 = 100 + 1/2\Delta b_1 \geqslant 0$$
$$\hat{X}_3 = 230 + 0 \cdot \Delta b_1 \geqslant 0$$
$$\hat{X}_6 = 20 + (-2)\Delta b_1 \geqslant 0$$
$$\hat{Z} = 1,350 + 1 \cdot \Delta b_1$$

Notes:

(1) The variables $\dot{X}_2$, $\dot{X}_3$, $\dot{X}_6$, and Z are the new values of the optimal basic variables and objective function obtained as a result of changing the first resource by Δb_1 (in the original problem).

(2) In relation 5.4, the coefficient of Δb_1, 1, gives the change in the optimal value of the objective function as a result of a unit increase in resource 1. This number, called the shadow price, indicates the value of an additional unit of resource. Thus, the shadow price, 1, signifies that the company should not pay more than $1 per additional unit of resource 1 ($1/minute of operation 1 time above the existing 430 minutes per day). If the company pays *less than* $1 per additional minute, then the company will make an additional net profit beyond $1350; if the company *actually* pays $1 per additional minute, then it will make no additional profits beyond $1350 (thus, $1 can be considered to be a break-even cost for additional operation 1 minutes); if the company pays more than $1 per additional minute of operation 1 time, then the company will have less than $1350 per-day profit even though it increased its resources. Clearly, it is uneconomical to pay more than $1 per additional minute ($60/hour) of operation 1 time.

(3) First, in relations 5.1, 5.2, and 5.3 above, nonnegativity of the variables (feasibility) is always required. (When *ranging objective function coefficients*, the range obtained maintains *optimality*; when *ranging resources*, the range obtained maintains *feasibility*.) Finally, the shadow price of $1 is only valid for the range obtained as a result of solving relations 5.1, 5.2, and 5.3. (If Δb_1 is outside of this range, then the shadow price will change from $1 to some other value. If Δb_1 is outside of the range obtained from relations 5.1-5.3, then at least one of the right-hand sides will become negative in the tableau; that is, the solution is infeasible but optimal, or *superoptimal*. Optimality can be maintained and feasibility can be restored by a procedure called the *Dual Simplex Method*, and in the process, the shadow price will generally change.

Solve relation 5.1 for Δb_1:

$$100 + 1/2\Delta b_1 \geq 0$$

gives

$$\Delta b_1 \geq -200 \qquad [5.5]$$

If relation 5.5 is satisfied, then $\dot{X}_2 \geq 0$. If $\Delta b_1 = -200$, then by relation 5.1 $\dot{X}_2 = 0$. Solving relation 5.2 for Δb_1 gives no additional information regarding Δb_1. Solving relation 5.3 for Δb_1,

$$20 - 2\Delta b_1 \geq 0$$

gives

$$\Delta b_1 \geq 10 \qquad\qquad [5.6]$$

In order to maintain feasibility, both relations 5.5 and 5.6 need to be satisfied simultaneously, that is, by relations 5.5 and 5.6:

$$-200 \leq \Delta b_1 \leq 10 \qquad\qquad [5.7]$$

Relation 5.7 gives the range that we were seeking to retain feasibility. Recall that Δb_1 is the change from the original right-hand value for constraint 1 (430). Denoting the actual value of this resource by b_1, we have that (from relation 5.7),

$$230 \leq b_1 \leq 440 \qquad\qquad [5.8]$$

Finally, by note 3,

$$Z = 1350 + 1\Delta b_1$$

where

$$-200 \leq \Delta b_1 \leq 10$$

so that

$$1150 \leq Z \leq 1360$$

PROBLEM

Range resources 2 and 3 as above. Note that the shadow price corresponding to resource 3 is zero and that X_6 is a slack variable. (This is a general property called *complementary slackness*. The shadow prices are *optimal dual variables*. Complementary slackness refers to the fact that product of the optimal dual variables with the corresponding optimal slack variables is equal to zero. Observe that for both constraints 1 and 2, the optimal slack variables are zero but the optimal dual variables are not zero.)

Example 2. A company that manufactures three products, A, B, and C, requiring two raw materials—labor and material—wants to determine the optimal production schedule that maximizes the total profit. The following linear program was formulated to answer this.

$$\text{maximize } Z = 3X_1 + X_2 + 5X_3$$
$$\text{subject to} \quad 6X_1 + 3X_2 + 5X_3 \leqslant 45 \text{ (labor)}$$
$$3X_1 + 4X_2 + 5X_3 \leqslant 30 \text{ (material)}$$
$$X_1, X_2, X_3 \geqslant 0$$

where X_1, X_2, and X_3 are the amounts of products A, B, and C, respectively, to produce. The computer prints out the following *optimal tableau* (X_4 and X_5 are slack variables).

PROBLEM

Solve by the Simplex Method to obtain the optimal solution in Tableau 5.2.

TABLEAU 5.2

	C_j	3	1	5	0	0	
C_B	Basis	X_1	X_2	X_3	X_4	X_5	Constants
3	X_1	1	-1/3	0	1/3	-1/3	5
5	X_3	0	1	1	-1/5	2/5	3
	$C_j - Z_j$	0	-3	0	0	-1	$Z = 30$

Observe that X_4 is nonbasic (the slack variable $X_4 = 0$) and the shadow price $Z_4 - C_4$ (optimal dual variable) is also zero. The variable X_4 can be put into the basis (entered) with no change in Z and X_1 will leave. The presence of a nonbasic variable with a relative profit of zero in the optimal tableau indicates an *alternate optimal solution*.

PROBLEM

(1) Find the range on the unit profits of products A and B.
   (*Hint:* Range the objective function coefficients of X_1 and X_2, where X_1 is a basic variable and X_2 is a nonbasic variable.)

(2) Suppose that an additional 15 units of material may be obtained at a cost of $10. Is it profitable to purchase *all* 15 units? Explain why or why not. (What about 16 units for $10?)
   (Answer to 2): Show that it *is* profitable to purchase all 15 units but no more than 15 more units. (*Hint:* Range the right-hand side of constraints; find the range for Δb_2 and show that $\Delta b_2 \leq 15$.)

6. COMPUTER SOLUTIONS TO
LINEAR PROGRAMMING PROBLEMS

The development of linear programming and the development of the digital computer have occurred simultaneously. The first linear programming problem that was solved on a computer was a U.S. Air Force problem in 1952 involving the development and support of aircraft subject to strategic and physical constraints on a machine (called SEAC) at the National Bureau of Standards. The large computer programs, called *LP codes* or *LP systems*, that are presently available to solve large-scale linear programs (hundreds of thousands of variables and tens of thousands of constraints) owe their efficiencies to the current generation of computers with their extremely large drums and disks in addition to their fast arithmetic operations. In addition, with advances in microcomputer hardware, some of the good linear programming software for microcomputers can solve problems with as many as thousands of variables and hundreds of constraints if the time to obtain a solution is not critical.

Input

In order to solve a general linear programming problem, it is necessary to input the problem type (maximization or minimization), the objective function coefficients, the constraint coefficients, the right-hand sides of the constraints, and whether each constraint is less than or equal to, equality, or greater than or equal to. It will not be assumed here that the reader is a computer programmer because the LP code illustrated here is "user friendly," meaning that the analyst needs only to follow the rules for input and subsequently be able to interpret the output based upon understanding linear programming concepts. Here, it is unnecessary to introduce slack, surplus, or artificial variables. This will be handled by the LP code, so that the analyst need only input the original model.

It is usual practice to specify a name, or mnemonic, to each variable and constraint. This practice provides for more descriptive output, especially when the names are actually mnemonics for the quantities that the variables and constraints represent.

Generally, the objective function is either (1) entered separately by giving the names of the variables and its objective function coefficients, or (2) it is entered as part of the constraints. In case 2, the coefficients are given the system-reserved constraint name OBJECT.

The right-hand sides are entered by giving the constraint name and the numerical value. Also, the type of relationship ($\leq$, $\geq$, or =) must be specified.

Because most LP codes are written in a combination of assembly language and FORTRAN, the input is restricted to formatting rules of these languages. This means that, among other things, the names must be keyed in specified columns of the input cards with no deviations allowed. Also, it means that all numbers must include decimal points.

Some LP codes do not require strict formatting rules for data entry; that is, there are programs that will allow free-form entry into the program. This will also eliminate the need to enter zero coefficients, which one usually must do with FORTRAN-based codes. One such computer code is LINDO from the University of Chicago and Scientific Press. LINDO also has friendly output code.

It should be noted that many codes allow the user to specify various error-correcting features (to control the growth of errors) and output formats. Also, they provide the capability of identifying the problem to the code and to the user by allowing the user to give a title to the problem that will be printed as a heading on each page of the output.

To illustrate the concepts discussed, consider the following simple example that was solved by a University of Minnesota program called LPKODE.

Example 1. Consider the following linear programming problem that is a model for maximizing profit from making feather beds.

$$\text{maximize } Z = 2X_1 + 11X_2$$
$$\text{subject to} \quad 2X_1 + 2X_2 \leq 20 \quad \text{(cutting design)}$$
$$X_1 + 2X_2 \leq 12 \quad \text{(finishing)}$$
$$3X_1 + 4X_2 \leq 36 \quad \text{(shaping)}$$
$$X_2 \leq 5 \quad \text{(feather limitation)}$$
$$X_1 \geq 0, \ X_2 \geq 0$$

PROBLEM

Solve by the Simplex Method and by the graphical method to verify the computer results. Also, perform sensitivity analysis on the objective function coefficients and right-hand sides to verify the computer results (solving this problem by hand will be useful to understanding the computer output that will follow).

Following is listed the input to LPKODE (see Figure 6.1). Note that this program allows one to enter interactively (on line) or by batch (with punched cards). In this case, the user chose to enter on line, so ORIGIN was entered. Next, the title was given as LP Example Model. Also, M (rows) gives the number of constraints (M = 4) and N (columns) gives the number of variables (N = 2). Print option (= –1) in LPKODE means to print only the first (initial) and last (optimal) tableaus. MAX/MIN? asks the problem type, so that the answer is MAX. ROW, COLUMN, AND MATRIX VALUES gives the objective function and constraint coefficients (row 0 is the objective function row—that is, constraint 00); so that 00 01 2. means that in row 00 (objective function), column (variable) 01 (X_1) has a coefficient of 2.; 00 02 11. means that the objective function coefficient (row 00) of X_2 (column 02) has a value of 11. Also, 01 01 2. means that the first constraint (row 01) has a coefficient of 2. for X_1 (column 01), and so on.

Now, ROW, TYPE, AND RHS VALUE asks for the type ($\leq$, $\geq$, or =) for each constraint and its right-hand side value. Thus, 01 lt 20. means that the first constraint is a less-than-or-equal-to constraint (some codes use .LE. rather than lt) and the right-hand side of the first constraint is 20. WHAT ROW (NN) AND NEW LABEL asks what name you want to give each constraint. Here constraint 1 is called "cutting," constraint 2 is called "finish," constraint 3 is called "shape," and constraint 4 is called "feather." WHAT COLUMN (NN) AND NEW LABEL asks what name you want to give to your variables. Here, X_1 (01) is called "child" and X_2 (02) is called "adult." Finally, you are asked if you want to revise your data (in case of input errors) and what the name of the file is where you want your data saved (ed file).

```
WELCOME TO LPKODE. VERSION
INPUT FILE NAME. IF ON LINE ENTER -ORIGIN-        ? origin
TITLE
? lp example model
  M - (ROWS)          ? 4
  N - (COLUMNS)       ? 2
  PRINT OPTION        ? -1
  MAX/MIN             ? max
  ROW, COLUMN, AND MATRIX VALUES
? 00012.
? 000211.
? 01012.
? 01022.
? 02011.
? 02022.
? 03013.
? 03024.
? 04021.
?
  ROW, TYPE, AND RHS VALUE
? 011t20.
? 021t12.
? 031t36.
? 041t5.
?
  WHAT ROW(NN) AND NEW LABEL
? 01cutting
? 02finish
? 03shape
? 04feather
?
  WHAT COLUMN(NN) AND NEW LABEL
? 01child
? 02adult
?
  DO YOU WANT TO REVISE YOUR DATA      ? no
  ON WHICH FILE DO YOU WANT YOUR DATA SAVED     ?edfile
```

Figure 6.1: LPKODE Input Program

Output

As we have seen in Chapter 5, there is a large amount of information about the solution to a linear programming problem that is contained in the optimal tableau. Typical output from an LP code will summarize the information from the optimal tableau in a useful form. It should be noted that some codes also allow for the option of having the output to be saved on disk or tape for future input to a report generator or else rerun the problem with slight variations.

The output will provide the problem heading, the number of iterations required, and the optimal value of the objective function. Also, it is usual to have a list of all of the variables that were originally specified, and an indication of which variables are basic. The value of each variable is provided in addition to the values of either $C_j - Z_j$ (or $Z_j - C_j$ in many LP codes).

The next part of the output gives the constraints and indicates whether each constraint is slack (loose) or binding (tight). If the computer code had to provide a slack, surplus, or artificial variable, the value of that variable is provided. Also, the dual variable value (the marginal cost of each additional resource unit) is provided by many LP codes.

Finally, ranges of values for each of the objective function coefficients and each of the right-hand-side values are given from sensitivity analysis of the optimal solution. As indicated in Chapter 5, the range obtained for a particular value assumes that no other values are changed.

Example 2. In this example, consider the output (output 1) from example 1 listed in Figure 6.2. Note that under MAX LP EXAMPLE Model (up to TERMINAL SOLUTION AFTER 2 ITERATIONS) the problem data (objective and constraint coefficients and right-hand sides) are displayed as an "echo check" to enable the analyst to confirm whether or not the original problem was entered correctly. Observe that our problem has been entered correctly. Next, we are informed that two iterations were required to obtain the optimal solution. The optimal solution is Z (total) = 59, and the optimal values of the original problem variables are X_1 (child) = 2, and X_2 (adult) = 5. Now, the computer code supplied X_3, X_4, X_5, and X_6 as slack variables, respectively, for the constraints named "cutting" (constraint 1), "finish" (constraint 2), "shape" (constraint 3), and "feather" (constraint 4). Further, the optimal values of the slack variables provided are $X_3 = 6$, $X_4 = 0$, $X_5 = 10$, and $X_6 = 0$, so that constraints 1 and 3 are nonbinding (loose or slack) and constraints 2 and 4 are binding (tight). In addition, the values of $Z_j - C_j$ (the negatives of the optimal values of the relative profits $C_j - Z_j$) are $Z_3 - C_3 = 0$, $Z_4 - C_4 = 2$, $Z_5 - C_5 = 0$, and $Z_6 - C_6 = 7$ (so that $C_3 - Z_3 = 0$, $C_4 - Z_4 = -2$, $C_5 - Z_5 = 0$, and $C_6 - Z_6 = -7$).

MAX   LP EXAMPLE MODEL

ROW	COL	VALUE	ROW	COL	VALUE	ROW	COL	VALUE
0	1	2.00000	0	2	11.0000	1	1	2.00000
1	2	2.00000	2	1	1.00000	2	2	2.00000
3	1	3.00000						
3	2	4.00000	4	2	1.00000			

ROW	TYPE	VALUE	ROW	TYPE	VALUE	ROW	TYPE	VALUE
1	LT	20.0000	2	LT	12.0000	3	LT	36.0000
4	LT	5.00000						
	CUTTING	FINISH	SHAPE	FEATHER				
	CHILD	ADULT						

TERMINAL SOLUTION AFTER 2 ITERATIONS

VARIABLE	QUANTITY	CURRENT PRICE	TOTAL	SHADOW PRICE
1CHILD	2.000	2.000	4.0000	0
2ADULT	5.000	11.000	55.0000	0
TOTAL			59.0000	

EQUATION	*******SLACK******* VARIABLE NUMBER	AMOUNT	SHADOW PRICE
CUTTING	3	6.0000	0
FINISH	4	0	2.000
SHAPE	5	10.0000	0
FEATHER	6	0	7.000

Figure 6.2: Output 1

Next, consider output 2 (postoptimality analysis) listed in Figure 6.3. First, the *objective function coefficients* are ranged only for the original variables X_1 (child) and X_2 (adult). Note that $0 \le C_1 \le 5.5$ where $C_1 = 2$ currently, and $4 \le C_2 < \infty$ where $C_2 = 11$ currently. If $C_1 < 0$ (minimum price), then X_4 enters and X_1 leaves; if $C_1 > 5.5$ (maximum price), then X_6 enters and X_3 leaves. If $C_2 < 4$ (minimum price) then X_6 enters and X_3 leaves; because C_2 cannot exceed infinity (.100E + 11 = 100 billion for computer purposes), no variables enter or leave as this is not possible.

Observe that for *right-hand side ranging*

$14 \le b_1 < \infty$ and if $b_1 < 14$, X_3 leaves;

$10 \le b_2 \le 15$ and if $b_2 < 10$, X_1 leaves; if $b_2 > 15$, X_3 leaves;

$26 \le b_3 < \infty$ and if $b_3 < 26$, X_5 leaves, and

$2 \le b_4 \le 6$ and if $b_4 < 2$, X_3 leaves; and if $b_4 > 6$, X_1 leaves.

Also, the original values of the resources are given as $b_1 = 20$, $b_2 = 12$, $b_3 = 36$, and $b_4 = 5$, so that we can compute the *changes* in the resources as

$$-6 \le \Delta b_1 < \infty,$$
$$-2 \le \Delta b_2 \le 3,$$
$$-10 \le \Delta b_3 < \infty,$$
$$-3 \le \Delta b_4 \le 1,$$

and knowing the shadow prices from output 1, we can compute the corresponding changes in the objective function values over each of the ranges in turn.

Finally, it was not desired to save the output on any file, to revise the problem, or to solve more problems. The execution time is given as .377 seconds of computer time.

POST OPTIMALITY ANALYSIS

VARIABLE	MINIMUM PRICE	VARIABLES AFFECTED IN OUT	QUANTITY	MAXIMUM PRICE	VARIABLES AFFECTED IN OUT	QUANTITY
1CHILD	0	4- 1	2.000	5.500	6- 3	3.000
2ADULT	4.000	6- 3	3.000*	.100E+11	0- 0	0

EQUATION	**********RIGHT HAND SIDE VALUES*********** ORIGINAL	MINIMUM	MAXIMUM
CUTTING	20.000	14.000 (3)	* .100E+11 (0)
FINISH	12.000	10.000 (1)	5.000 (3)
SHAPE	36.000	26.000 (5)	* .100E+11 (0)
FEATHER	5.000	2.000 (3)	6.000 (1)

Figure 6.3: Postoptimality analysis   *(continued)*

```
ON WHICH FILE DO YOU WANT YOUR OUTPUT SAVED        ? none

.377 SECONDS OF COMPUTER TIME USED
REVISE THIS PROBLEM ? no
MORE PROBLEMS       ? no
READY.
```

Figure 6.3 Continued

PROBLEMS

(1) If you have access to a computer linear programming (LP) code, then solve examples 1, 3, and 4 from Chapter 2. Compare the computer results of example 3 with those obtained in Chapters 4 and 5. Furthermore, if you have access to an LP code with integer programming capabilities, use the integer option to solve example 5 of Chapter 2.

(2) Relax-and-Enjoy, a land development corporation, is developing a lakeside resort at a privately owned lake and is in the business of selling property for vacation and/or retreat cottages. An advertising firm has been hired to promote this project. This firm has come up with five possible advertising media for the first month's promotional campaign. The effectiveness, cost, and availability of each media is given in Table 6.1.

Relax-and-Enjoy's objective is to maximize the total expected exposure units of their advertisement campaign. Their advertising budget is exactly $30,000 for the first month. They would like to have at least ten TV commercials during the month, but want to limit the expenses on TV commercials to $18,000. Finally, they want to ensure that at least 50,000 potential families are reached by their promotional campaign. This situation can be formulated as a linear programming model as follows:

let DTV = number of times daytime TV is used,
    ETV = number of times evening TV is used,
    DNP = number of times daily newspaper is used,
    SNP = number of times Sunday newspaper is used, and
    RAD = number of times radio is used.

maximize $Z = 65\text{DTV} + 90\text{ETV} + 40\text{DNP} + 60\text{SNP} + 20\text{RAD}$
(total exposure units for the entire campaign)

subject to   DTV .LE. 15 (maximum availability of daytime TV)
                ETV .LE. 10 (maximum availability of evening TV)
                DNP .LE. 25 (maximum availability of daily paper)
                SNP .LE. 4 (maximum availability of Sunday paper)
                RAD .LE. 30 (maximum availability of radio)

TABLE 6.1
Effectiveness, Cost, and Availability of Media

Media	Number Of Potential Families Reached	Cost Per Run Of Their Commercial	Maximum Times Available Per Month	Expected Exposure Units
Daytime TV	1,000	$1,500	15	65
Evening TV	2,000	$3,000	10	90
Daily Paper	1,500	$ 400	25	40
Sunday Paper	2,500	$1,000	4	60
Radio	300	$ 100	30	20

1500DTV + 300ETV + 400DNP + 1000SNP + 100RAD .EQ. 30000 (budget $)
DTV + ETV .GE. 10 (minimum usage of TV)
1000DTV + 2000ETV + 1500DNP + 2500SNP + 300RAD .GE. 50000
(minimum families reached by the campaign)
DTV, ETV, DNP, SNP, and RAD .GE. 0 (nonnegativity)

This problem was solved using MPOS (Multi-Purpose Optimization System, developed at Northwestern University), shown in Figure 6.4. Use the output to answer the following questions:

(1) State the optimal advertising strategy for Relax-and-Enjoy. What is the total units of expected exposure for this campaign?
(2) If Relax-and-Enjoy insisted on putting up one commercial on the evening television during the first month, what would happen to the current optimal advertising strategy? What would be the total expected exposure then?
(3) When would it be worthwhile to advertise on evening television?
(4) If Relax-and-Enjoy had $31,500 for the first month's advertising expenses (instead of $30,000), what would happen to the current optimal *basic* strategy? What would be the total expected exposures then?
(5) Relax-and-Enjoy initially desired that at least 50,000 potential families must be reached. Within what range can this requirement vary without altering the current basic optimal advertising plan?

68

```
REGULAR
TITLE
ADVERTISEMENT MEDIA SELECTION PROBLEM
*DTV = NUMBER OF TIMES DAY TV IS USED
*ETV = NUMBER OF TIMES EVENING TV IS USED
*DNP = NUMBER OF TIMES DAILY NEWSPAPER IS USED
*SNP = NUMBER OF TIMES SUNDAY NEWSPAPER IS USED
*RAD = NUMBER OF TIMES RADIO IS USED
MAXIMIZE
65DTV + 90ETV + 40DNP + 60SNP + 20RAD
CONSTRAINTS
1.  DTV .LE. 15
2.  ETV .LE. 10
3.  DNP .LE. 25
4.  SNP .LE. 4
5.  RAD .LE. 30
6.  1500DTV + 3000ETV + 400DNP + 1000SNP + 100RAD .EQ. 30000
7.  DTV + ETV .GE. 10
8.  1500DTV + 3000ETV .LE. 18000
9.  1000DTV + 2000ETV + 1500DNP + 2500SNP + 300RAD .GE. 50000
RNGOBJ
RNGRHS
OPTIMIZE
```

SUMMARY OF RESULTS

VAR NO	VAR NAME	ROW NO	STATUS	ACTIVITY LEVEL	OPPORTUNITY COST	LOWER BOUND	UPPER BOUND
1	DTV	--	B	10.0000000	0.0000000	0.0000	INF
2	ETV	--	LB	0.0000000	65.0000000	0.0000	INF
3	DNP	--	B	25.0000000	0.0000000	0.0000	INF
4	SNP	--	B	2.0000000	0.0000000	0.0000	INF
5	RAD	--	B	30.0000000	0.0000000	0.0000	INF
6	SLACK-- B- 1		B	5.0000000	0.0000000	0.0000	INF
7	SLACK-- B- 2		B	10.0000000	0.0000000	0.0000	INF
8	SLACK-- B- 3		LB	0.0000000	16.0000000	0.0000	INF
9	SLACK-- B- 4		B	2.0000000	0.0000000	0.0000	INF
10	SLACK-- B- 5		LB	0.0000000	14.0000000	0.0000	INF
11	ARTIF-- B- 6		LB	0.0000000	.0600000	0.0000	INF
12	SLACK-- 7		LB	0.0000000	25.0000000	0.0000	INF
21	ARTIF-- B- 7		LB	0.0000000	-25.0000000	0.0000	INF
13	SLACK-- B- 8		B	3000.0000000	0.0000000	0.0000	INF
14	SLACK-- 9		B	11500.0000000	0.0000000	0.0000	INF
23	ARTIF-- B- 9		LB	0.0000000	0.0000000	0.0000	INF

MAXIMUM VALUE OF THE OBJECTIVE FUNCTION = 2370.000000

RNGRHS
******
(OPTIMALITY RANGE FOR RIGHT-HAND-SIDE CONSTANTS)
NON-SLACK RESOURCES ONLY

RNGOBJ
******
(OPTIMALITY RANGE FOR COST COEFFICIENTS)
BASIC VARIABLES ONLY

BI	XOUT	MIN BI / Z-LOWER	ORIGINAL BI / Z	MAX BI / Z-UPPER	XOUT	CJ	XIN	MIN CJ / Z-LOWER	ORIGINAL CJ / Z	MAX CJ / Z-UPPER	XIN
3	9	20.000 / 2290.0	25.000 / 2370.0	30.000 / 2450.0	4	4	12	43.333 / 2336.7	60.000 / 2370.0	100.00 / 2450.0	
5	9	10.000 / 2090.0	30.000 / 2370.0	50.000 / 2650.0	4	1	2	.18190E-11 / 1720.0	65.000 / 2370.0	90.000 / 2620.0	12
6	4	28000. / 2250.0	30000. / 2370.0	32000. / 2490.0	9	5	10	6.0000 / 1950.0	20.000 / 2370.0	*INF*	
7	9	8.6667 / 2403.3	10.000 / 2370.0	11.333 / 2336.7	4	3	8	24.000 / 1970.0	40.000 / 2370.0	*INF*	

Figure 6.4: Relax-and-Enjoy's Linear Programming Model

(6) If the exposure of a commercial in the daily newspaper was 60 instead of 40, what would happen to the current optimal advertising strategy? What would be the total expected exposure of the campaign then?

(7) What would be the specific consequences if the unit exposure of a commercial in the Sunday newspaper was only 40 (instead of 60)?

(8) What would be the specific consequences if Relax-and-Enjoy was prepared to spend $40,000 on the first month's campaign, instead of $30,000?

Compare the input form of MPOS with that of LPKODE. Observe that the form of input in MPOS is identical to that of the model. The term REGULAR refers to the ordinary Simplex Method for continuous linear programming (not integer programming, although MPOS has an integer option); RNGOBJ refers to ranging the objective function coefficients; RNGRHS refers to ranging the right-hand sides; and OPTIMIZE results in the execution of the algorithm.

For output, observe that STATUS refers to B (Basic) or LB (Non-basic), ACTIVITY LEVEL is the numerical value of the variable (e.g., DTV = 10 and ETV = 0), and OPPORTUNITY COST is the $Z_j-C_j=-\bar{C}_j$ associated with that variable. Finally, right-hand side ranging is done only when that constraint is tight (binding) and objective function coefficients are ranged for basic variables only.

APPENDIX 1:
PROPERTIES OF LINEAR
PROGRAMMING PROBLEMS

Convex Sets

Suppose that *any* two points, $\dot{X}_1$ and $\dot{X}_2$, are chosen from a closed region R. If these points are connected by a straight line segment and all of the points lying on this straight line segment are also contained in R, then the collection of points is called a *convex set*—that is, let $\dot{X}_1$, $\dot{X}_2$ be *any* two points contained in a closed region R. If all points $\dot{X}$, where

$$\dot{X} = \beta\dot{X}_1 + (1-\beta)\dot{X}_2, \quad 0 \leqslant \beta \leqslant 1 \qquad [1]$$

lie within R for all $\dot{X}_1$ and $\dot{X}_2$, then the collection of points within R is a *convex set*.

If a point $\dot{X}$ of a convex set cannot be expressed as a linear combination of two other points from the convex set as in equation 1, then such a point is called an *extreme point*.

Example: Vertices of polygons are extreme points.

A point $\dot{X}$ that is a combination of points $\dot{X}_1, \dot{X}_2, \ldots, \dot{X}_R$ in a convex set; that is,

$$\hat{X} = \sum_{i=1}^{R} \mu_i \hat{X}_i, \quad \mu_i \geqslant 0, \quad i = 1, \ldots, R \qquad [2]$$

where

$$\sum_{i=1}^{R} \mu_i = 1 \qquad [3]$$

is called a *convex combination*. Such a point, $\hat{X}$, is also a member of the convex set. The region containing all convex combinations of a *finite* number of points $\hat{X}_1, \hat{X}_2, \ldots, \hat{X}_R$ is called a *convex polyhedron*.

Hyperplanes

Consider an equation for a hyperplane in n-space, that is,

$$d_1 X_1 + d_2 X_2 + \ldots + d_n X_n = b \qquad [4]$$

or

$$\hat{D}^T \hat{X} = b \qquad [5]$$

where

$$\hat{D} = \begin{bmatrix} d_1 \\ d_2 \\ \vdots \\ d_n \end{bmatrix} \qquad [6]$$

Choose any two points $\hat{X}_1, \hat{X}_2$ on the hyperplane, that is,

$$\hat{D}^T \hat{X}_1 = b$$

$$\hat{D}^T \hat{X}_2 = b$$

and form the convex combination

$$\hat{X} = \beta \hat{X}_1 + (1 - \beta) \hat{X}_2, \quad 0 < \beta < 1 \qquad [7]$$

Then, by equation 7,

$$\hat{D}^T \hat{X} = D^T [\beta \hat{X}_1 + (1 - \beta) \hat{X}_2] \qquad [8]$$

$$= \beta \hat{D}^T \hat{X}_1 + (1 - \beta) D^T \hat{X}_2$$

$$= \beta b + (1 - \beta) b = b$$

so that $\tilde{X}$ is also on the hyperplane, and thus $S = \{\tilde{X} : \tilde{D}^T \tilde{X} = b\}$ is a convex set.

Consider a point $\tilde{X}_1$ that lies on the hyperplane, $\tilde{D}^T \tilde{X}_1 = b$, and a point $\tilde{X}_2$ that lies in the half-space above the hyperplane, $\tilde{D}^T \tilde{X}_2 > b$. Then, forming $\tilde{X}$ as in equation 7,

$$\tilde{D}^T \tilde{X} = \tilde{D}^T [\beta \tilde{X}_1 + (1 - \beta) \tilde{X}_2]$$

$$= \beta \tilde{D}^T \tilde{X}_1 + (1 - \beta) \tilde{D}^T \tilde{X}_2 > \beta b + (1 - \beta) b = b$$

that is,

$$\tilde{D}^T \tilde{X} > b \tag{9}$$

so that $\tilde{X}$ lies above the hyperplane.

Notes

(1) It has been shown that (a) a hyperplane is a convex set and that (b) a half-space above or below a hyperplane is a convex set.

(2) It is not difficult to show that (a) the space enclosed by the intersection of two or more hyperplanes is a convex set and that (b) the intersection of two or more half-spaces is a convex set.

Feasible Solutions

Consider the linear programming problem

maximize (or minimize) $Z = \tilde{C}^T \tilde{X}$

subject to $A\tilde{X} = \tilde{B}$

$X \geqslant 0$

where

$$A = [\tilde{P}_1, \tilde{P}_2, \ldots, \tilde{P}_{n+m}],$$

$$\tilde{P}_j = \begin{bmatrix} a_{1j} \\ a_{2j} \\ \vdots \\ a_{mj} \end{bmatrix}$$

$$\tilde{B} = \begin{bmatrix} b_1 \\ \vdots \\ b_m \end{bmatrix}$$

Note: The constraints $A\tilde{X} = \tilde{B}$ can be written as

$$X_1 \tilde{P}_1 + X_2 \tilde{P}_2 + \ldots + X_{n+m} \tilde{P}_{n+m} = \tilde{B}$$

Now, it can be seen that an equality constraint

$$a_{i1} X_1 + a_{i2} X_2 + \ldots + a_{i, n+m} X_{n+m} = b_i$$

in the linear programming problem is a hyperplane of the form in equation 4. The set of equality constraints represents the intersection of a set of hyperplanes and is thus a convex set. In addition, a linear programming problem that contains both inequality and equality constraints yields a convex set *if* the half-spaces all intersect. Thus, a properly posed linear programming problem will result in feasible solutions that are contained in a closed convex set. Furthermore, this convex set will be a convex polyhedron if the number of constraints is finite and the set is bounded.

At this point, form the convex combination of feasible solutions $\tilde{X}_1$, $\tilde{X}_2, \ldots, \tilde{X}_R$; that is,

$$\tilde{X} = \mu_1 \tilde{X}_1 + \mu_2 \tilde{X}_2 + \ldots + \mu_R \tilde{X}_R, \ \mu_i \geq 0, \ i = 1, \ldots, R \qquad [10]$$

and

$$\mu_1 + \mu_2 + \ldots + \mu_R = 1 \qquad [11]$$

Forming the product $A\tilde{X}$, using equation 10 and $A\tilde{X}_i = \tilde{B}$, gives

$$A\tilde{X} = A[\mu_1 \tilde{X}_1 + \mu_2 \tilde{X}_2 + \ldots + \mu_R \tilde{X}_R]$$

$$= \mu_1 A\tilde{X}_1 + \mu_2 A\tilde{X}_2 + \ldots + \mu_R A\tilde{X}_R$$

$$= \mu_1 \tilde{B} + \mu_2 \tilde{B} + \ldots + \mu_R \tilde{B}$$

$$= (\mu_1 + \mu_2 + \ldots + \mu_R)\tilde{B} = 1\tilde{B} = \tilde{B},$$

that is,

$$A\tilde{X} = \tilde{B} \qquad [12]$$

where $\tilde{X}$ is given in equation 10.

It has been shown that *a convex combination of feasible solutions of a linear programming problem is also a feasible solution. Thus, the collection of all feasible solutions to a linear programming problem is a convex set.*

Optimal Feasible Solutions

Let $\check{X}_1, \check{X}_2, \ldots, \check{X}_R$ be the *extreme* points of a closed and bounded convex set, and let $\check{X}^*$ be *minimum (maximum) feasible solution*. Assume that $\check{X}^*$ is *not* an extreme point. Then, $\check{X}^*$ can be written as a convex combination of the extreme points $\check{X}_i$, $i = 1, \ldots, R$, that is,

$$\check{X}^* = \sum_{i=1}^{R} \mu_i \check{X}_i, \ \mu_i \geqslant 0, \ i = 1, \ldots, R \qquad [13]$$

and

$$\sum_{i=1}^{R} \mu_i = 1 \qquad [14]$$

and the objective function can be written as (by equation 13)

$$\check{C}^T \check{X}^* = \check{C}^T \left(\sum_{i=1}^{R} \mu_i \check{X}_i^i \right) = \sum_{i=1}^{R} \mu_i \check{C}^T \check{X}_i \qquad [15]$$

Then, replace each of the $\check{X}_i$ in equation 15 with that particular $\check{X}_j$ that gives the minimum value of $\check{C}^T \check{X}_i$, $1 \leqslant j \leqslant R$; that is,

$$C^T X^* \geqslant C^T X_j \qquad [16]$$

As X^* is given as the minimum feasible solution

$$\check{C}^T \check{X}^* \leqslant \check{C}^T \check{X}_j \qquad [17]$$

By relations 16 and 17,

$$\check{C}^T \check{X}^* = \check{C}^T \check{X}_j \qquad [18]$$

Thus, by equation 18, $\check{X}_j$, an *extreme point* of the convex set, is a minimum feasible solution.

Notes:

(1) The same type of reasoning can be applied to a maximum feasible solution. (Do this).

(2) Thus, the following principle is obtained: *feasible solutions that optimize the given objective function are extreme points of the convex set.*

Now assume that $\check{X}_1, \check{X}_2, \ldots, \check{X}_R$ are feasible solutions that optimize the objective function, that is,

$$\check{C}^T\check{X}_1 = \check{C}^T\check{X}_2 = \ldots = \check{C}^T\check{X}_R \qquad [19]$$

Then, form the convex combination

$$\check{X} = \sum_{i=1}^{R} \mu_i\check{X}_i, \; \mu_i \geqslant 0, \; i = 1, \ldots, R \qquad [20]$$

and

$$\sum_{i=1}^{R} \mu_i = 1 \qquad [21]$$

Then, the objective function is

$$\check{C}^T\check{X} = \sum_{i=1}^{R} \mu_i\check{C}^T\check{X}_i \qquad [22]$$

By equation 19, as all $\check{C}^T\check{X}_i$ on the right-hand side of equation 22 are equal, replace each of these terms with any term, say $\check{C}^T\check{X}_j$, so that

$$\check{C}^T\check{X} = \sum_{i=1}^{R} \mu_i\check{C}^T\check{X}_j = \check{C}^T\check{X}_j \sum_{i=1}^{R} \mu_i = (\check{C}^T\check{X}_j)(1) = \check{C}^T\check{X}_j \qquad [23]$$

Thus, by equation 23, if the objective function is optimized at *more than one point*, then the objective function takes on the same optimal value at any convex combination of the extreme points.

Recall that a set of vectors $\bar{y}_1, \bar{y}_2, \ldots, \bar{y}_R$ are linearly independent if and only if the linear combination $\alpha_1\bar{y}_1 + \ldots + \alpha_R\bar{y}_R = \bar{0}$ holds only for $\alpha_1 = \alpha_2 = \ldots = \alpha_R = 0$.

Note: Linear independence implies that no single vector $\bar{y}_i$ can be written as a linear combination of the remaining $R-1$ vectors. At this point, consider the expression

$$X_1\check{P}_1 + X_2\check{P}_2 + \ldots + X_R\check{P}_R = \check{P}_0 \qquad [24]$$

where $X_i \geqslant 0, \; i = 1, 2, \ldots, R$; the vectors $\check{P}_1, \check{P}_2, \ldots, \check{P}_R$ are linearly independent; and R is the number of linearly independent vectors required to represent the given vector $\check{P}_0$, where $R \leqslant m$.

Note: Recall that equation 24 is one way to express the constraints of a linear programming problem. It can be shown that *the number of non-zero components of any basic feasible solution vector cannot exceed m, the number of rows (constraints) in the constraint matrix.*

Write the constraints in terms of $\check{X}_1$ and $\check{X}_2$ as

$$A\check{X}_1 = \check{B} \qquad [25]$$

and

$$A\check{X}_2 = \check{B} \qquad [26]$$

or, in vector notation,

$$X_{11}\check{P}_1 + X_{21}\check{P}_2 + \ldots + X_{R1}\check{P}_R = \check{P}_0 \qquad [27]$$

$$X_{12}\check{P}_1 + X_{22}\check{P}_2 + \ldots + X_{R2}\check{P}_R = \check{P}_0 \qquad [28]$$

Subtracting equation 28 from equation 27 gives

$$(X_{11} - X_{12})\check{P}_1 + (X_{21} - X_{22})\check{P}_2 + \ldots + (X_{R1} - X_{R2})\check{P}_R = \check{0} \qquad [29]$$

Because the vectors $\check{P}_1, \check{P}_2, \ldots, \check{P}_R$ are linearly independent, then

$$(X_{i1} - X_{i2}) = 0, \quad i = 1, \ldots, R$$

so that

$$X_{i1} = X_{i2}$$

or

$$\check{X}_1 = \check{X}_2 = \check{X} \qquad [30]$$

Because $\check{X}$ cannot be expressed as a convex combination of two *distinct* feasible solutions (as $\check{X}$ is an extreme point), it is concluded that *the n-dimensional vector whose nonzero elements are the coefficients of the expression*

$$X_1\check{P}_1 + X_2\check{P}_2 + \ldots + X_R\check{P}_R = \check{P}_0$$

$$X_i \geqslant 0, \quad i = 1, \ldots, R$$

and $R \leqslant m$, is an extreme point of the convex set of all feasible solutions if $\check{P}_1, \check{P}_2, \ldots, \check{P}_R$ are linearly independent.

Assume now that $\check{X}$ is an extreme point of the convex set of all feasible solutions and that $X_i > 0$, $i = 1, 2, \ldots, R$ and $X_i = 0$, $i = R + 1, \ldots, n$. Consider the expression

$$X_1\check{P}_1 + X_2\check{P}_2 + \ldots + X_R\check{P}_R = \check{P}_0 \qquad [31]$$

At this point, assume that $\check{P}_1, \check{P}_2, \ldots, \check{P}_R$ are *linearly dependent*. Then, for the expression

$$\mu_1 \check{P}_1 + \mu_2 \check{P}_2 + \ldots + \mu_R\check{P}_R = 0 \qquad [32]$$

at least one $\mu_i = 0$. Also,

$$X_1 \check{P}_1 + X_2 \check{P}_2 + \ldots + X_R \check{P}_R = \check{P}_0 \qquad [33]$$

Multiplying both sides of equation 32 by $\epsilon > 0$ and then adding and then subtracting gives the following two expressions

$$(X_1 + \epsilon \mu_1) \check{P}_1 + (X_2 + \epsilon \mu_2) \check{P}_2 + \ldots + (X_R + \epsilon \mu_R) \check{P}_R = \check{P}_0 \qquad [34]$$

and

$$(X_1 - \epsilon \mu_1) \check{P}_1 + (X_2 - \epsilon \mu_2) \check{P}_2 + \ldots + (X_R - \epsilon \mu_R) \check{P}_R = \check{P}_0 \qquad [35]$$

Choose $\epsilon > 0$ sufficiently small so that all of the coefficients in equation 35 are nonnegative. Thus, if

$$\check{X}^1 = \begin{bmatrix} X_1 + \epsilon \mu_1 \\ X_2 + \epsilon \mu_2 \\ \vdots \\ X_R + \epsilon \mu_R \end{bmatrix}, \quad \check{X}^{11} = \begin{bmatrix} X_1 - \epsilon \mu_1 \\ X_2 - \epsilon \mu_2 \\ \vdots \\ X_R - \epsilon \mu_R \end{bmatrix} \qquad [36]$$

then both $\check{X}^1$ and $\check{X}^{11}$ are feasible solutions, where $\check{X}^1$, $\check{X}^{11}$, and $\check{X}$, the given extreme point, can be expressed as the convex combination

$$\check{X} = 1/2(X^1 + \check{X}^{11}) = 1/2 \check{X}^1 + 1/2 \check{X}^{11} \qquad [37]$$

However, equation 37 violates the assumption that $\check{X}$ is an extreme point. Therefore, the vectors $\check{P}_1$, $\check{P}_2$, ..., $\check{P}_R$ cannot be linearly dependent; that is, $\check{P}_1$, $\check{P}_2$, ..., $\check{P}_R$ must be linearly independent. Moreover, it is required that $R \leqslant m$, because the vectors $\check{P}_1$, $\check{P}_2$, ..., $\check{P}_R$ are m-dimensional, as is $\check{P}_0$, and the vector $\check{P}_0$ cannot be expressed in terms of more than m linearly independent vectors. Hence, the number of nonzero members of the extreme point $\check{X}$ cannot exceed m, the number of constraints. Thus, to summarize, *the vectors $\check{P}_1$, $\check{P}_2$, ..., $\check{P}_R$ in the expression $X_1 \check{P}_1 + X_2 \check{P}_2 + \ldots + X_R \check{P}_R$ are linearly independent, provided that $\check{X}$ is an extreme point of the convex set of all feasible solutions. Furthermore, not more than m elements of $\check{X}$ can be greater than zero.*

Notes:

(1) It has been shown that the solution to a linear programming problem is an extreme point of a convex set if a solution exists.

(2) Moreover, the solution vector will have no more than m linearly independent vectors associated with it, where m is the number of constraints.

(3) What is desired is a systematic method that successively will choose adjacent extreme points such that the objective function monotonically increases (for maximization problems) or decreases (for minimization problems). The *Simplex Algorithm* is such a procedure.

Development of the Simplex Algorithm

The problem is to find the particular subset of R linearly independent vectors, where $R \leqslant m$, out of the set of n vectors $\bar{P}_1, \bar{P}_2, \ldots, \bar{P}_n$ whose associated values of X_i, where

$$X_1 \bar{P}_1 + X_2 \bar{P}_2 + \ldots + X_R \bar{P}_R = \bar{P}_0, \quad R \leqslant m \qquad [1]$$

will cause the objective function

$$Z = \bar{C}^T \bar{X} \qquad [2]$$

to be optimized subject to the given constraints.

At this point, assume that the objective function 1 is to be minimized. Furthermore, assume that every extreme point $\bar{X}$ has exactly R = m linearly independent vectors associated with it.

Changing a Basis Vector–Feasibility

Assume that there exists a set of linearly independent vectors $\bar{P}_1$, $\bar{P}_2, \ldots, \bar{P}_m$ such that

$$X_{10} \bar{P}_1 + X_{20} \bar{P}_2 + \ldots + X_{m0} \bar{P}_m = \bar{P}_0 \qquad [3]$$

where the X_{i0} are the positive components of a given extreme point $\bar{X}_0$. Any other vector, say $\bar{P}_j$, of the original set of n vectors can be expressed as a linear combination of the given m vectors as

$$\bar{P}_j = X_{1j} \bar{P}_1 + X_{2j} \bar{P}_2 + \ldots + X_{mj} \bar{P}_m \qquad [4]$$

where X_{ij} is the ith component of $\bar{P}_j$, and at least one $X_{ij} = 0$. In other words, the given set of m linear independent vectors forms a *basis* for the m-dimensional vector space.

At this point, replace one of the basis vectors in equation 3, say $\bar{P}_\varrho$, with $\bar{P}_j$. Then solve equation 4 for $\bar{P}_\varrho$ where $X_{\varrho j} \neq 0$, that is,

$$\tilde{P}_\ell = 1/X_{\ell j}[\tilde{P}_j - X_{1j}\tilde{P}_1 - X_{2j}\tilde{P}_2 - \ldots - X_{\ell-1},_j \tilde{P}_{\ell-1} - X_{\ell+1} \quad [5]$$

$$_j \tilde{P}_{\ell+1} - \ldots - X_{mj}\tilde{P}_m].$$

Substituting equation 5 into equation 3 gives

$$X_{10}\tilde{P}_1 + X_{20}\tilde{P}_2 + \ldots + X_{\ell-1},_0 \tilde{P}_{\ell-1} + X_{\ell+1},_0 \tilde{P}_{\ell+1} + \ldots + \quad [6]$$

$$X_{m0}\tilde{P}_m + X_{\ell 0}/X_{\ell j}[\tilde{P}_j - X_{1j}\tilde{P}_1 - X_{2j}\tilde{P}_2 - \ldots - X_{\ell-1},$$

$$_j\tilde{P}_{\ell-1} - X_{\ell+1},_j\tilde{P}_{\ell+1} - \ldots - X_{mj}\tilde{P}_m] = P_0.$$

By grouping terms in equation 6, the following is obtained:

$$[X_{10} - X_{1j}(X_{\ell 0}/X_{\ell j})]\,\tilde{P}_1 + [X_{20} - X_{2j}(X_{\ell 0}/X_{\ell j})]\,\tilde{P}_2 + \ldots + \cdot \quad [7]$$

$$[X_{\ell-1,0} - X_{\ell-1,j}(X_{\ell 0}/X_{\ell j})]\,\tilde{P}_{\ell-1} + [X_{\ell+1,0} - X_{\ell+1,j}(X_{\ell 0}/X_{\ell j})]$$

$$\tilde{P}_{\ell+1} + \ldots + [X_{m0} - X_{mj}(X_{\ell 0}/X_{\ell j})]\,\tilde{P}_m + (X_{\ell 0}/X_{\ell j})\tilde{P}_j = \tilde{P}_0$$

Notes:

(1) Equation 7 expresses vector $\tilde{P}_0$ in terms of m vectors once again, but the original vector $\tilde{P}_\ell$ has been replaced by $\tilde{P}j$.

(2) Also, equation 7 indicates that the coefficients of the vectors are different. Observe that the new vectors are linearly independent, because if they were linearly dependent, then they could be written as

$$\alpha_1\tilde{P}_1 + \alpha_2\tilde{P}_2 + \ldots \alpha_{\ell-1}\tilde{P}_{\ell-1} + \alpha_{\ell+1} + \alpha_{\ell+1}\tilde{P}_{\ell+1} + \ldots + \quad [8]$$

$$\alpha_m\tilde{P}_m + \alpha_j\tilde{P}_j = \tilde{0}$$

where at least one of the $\alpha_i \neq 0$. Then, solving equation 8 for P_j, $\alpha_j \neq 0$,

$$\tilde{P}_j = -1/\alpha_j[\alpha_1\tilde{P}_1 + \alpha_2\tilde{P}_2 + \ldots \alpha_{\ell-1}\tilde{P}_{\ell-1} + \quad [9]$$

$$\alpha_{\ell+1}\tilde{P}_{\ell+1} + \ldots + \alpha_m\tilde{P}_m]$$

Subtract equation 9 from equation 4 to get

$$[X_{1j} - (\alpha_1/\alpha_j)]\,\tilde{P}_1 + [X_{2j} - (\alpha_2/\alpha_j)]\,\tilde{P}_2 + \ldots + \quad [10]$$

$$[X_{\ell-1,j} - (\alpha_{\ell-1}/\alpha_j)]\,\tilde{P}_{\ell-1} + X_{\ell j}\tilde{P}_\ell +$$

$$[X_{\ell+1,j} - (\alpha_{\ell+1}/\alpha_j)]\,\tilde{P}_{\ell+1} + \ldots + [X_{mj} - (\alpha_m/\alpha_j)]\,\tilde{P}_m = \tilde{0}$$

However, the vectors $\bar{P}_1, \bar{P}_2, \ldots, \bar{P}_m$ in equation 10 were defined as being linearly independent, and it was stated that $X_{\varrho j} \neq 0$. This is a contradiction to the statement that the vectors appearing in equation 7 are linearly dependent, and the vectors in equation 7 form a new basis for the m-dimensional vector space.

At this point, there is a new set of m linearly independent vectors, having coefficients (in equation 7) that are the elements of a new extreme point of the feasible set if each of the coefficients is positive; that is,

$$[X_{i0} - X_{ij}(X_{\varrho 0}/X_{\varrho j})] > 0, \quad i = 1, 2, \ldots, \ell - 1, \ell + 1, \ldots, m \quad [11]$$

and

$$X_{\varrho 0}/X_{\varrho j} > 0 \quad [12]$$

where equations 11 and 12 are written as strict inequalities as it is required that P_0 be written in terms of exactly m linearly independent vectors.

It is required that $X_{\varrho j} > 0$ to satisfy equation 12. If $X_{ij} \leqslant 0$ for $i \neq \ell$, then all coefficients given by equation 11 will always be positive. If $X_{ij} > 0$ for $i \neq \ell$, equation 11 will be satisfied as long as

$$X_{\varrho 0}/X_{\varrho j} < X_{i0}/X_{ij} \quad [13]$$

Thus, the vector $\bar{P}_\varrho$, eliminated from the original basis, is not arbitrary, but is that vector giving a minimum value for $X_{\varrho 0}/X_{\varrho j}$ based on equations 12 and 13.

Notes:

(1) One of the vectors in the original basis was replaced with one of the $(n - m)$ vectors originally not in the basis.

(2) The coefficients of the expression for $\bar{P}_0$ in terms of the new basis are the nonzero components of a new extreme point of the convex set of all feasible solutions.

(3) Expression 13 is the *minimum ratio rule*, where $X_{\varrho 0}$ is the right-hand side of constraint ℓ and $X_{\varrho j}$ is the pivot element.

Changing the Objective Function—Optimality

Now, examine the effect of the previous vector substitution on the objective function. Assume that the function

$$X_{10}C_1 + X_{20}C_2 + \ldots + X_{m0}C_m = Z_0 \quad [14]$$

is the objective function value that corresponds to equation 3, and assume that by equation 4, a vector, $\check{P}_j$, can be expressed in terms of the original basis vectors. Then the function

$$X_{1j}C_1 + X_{2j}C_2 + \ldots + X_{mj}C_m = Z_j \qquad [15]$$

may be considered to be *the equivalent cost of a unit of j* (or, *imputed cost*). Now, eliminate one of the coefficients, say C_ϱ, from equations 14 and 15. First, solve equation 15 for C_ϱ:

$$C_\varrho = 1/X_{\varrho j}(Z_j - X_{1j}C_1 - X_{2j}C_2 - \ldots - X_{\varrho-1,j}C_{\varrho-1} -$$

$$X_{\varrho-1,j}C_{\varrho+1} - \ldots - X_{mj}C_m)$$

and substituting into equation 14 gives

$$X_{10}C_1 + X_{20}C_2 + \ldots + X_{\varrho-1,0}C_{\varrho-1} + X_{\varrho+1,0}C_{\varrho+1} + \ldots +$$

$$X_{m0}C_m + X_{\varrho0}/X_{\varrho j}(Z_j - X_{1j}C_1 - X_{2j}C_2 - \ldots - X_{\varrho-1,j}C_{\varrho-1} -$$

$$X_{\varrho+1,j}C_{\varrho+1} - \ldots - X_{mj}C_m) = Z_0$$

and after grouping terms,

$$[X_{10} - X_{1j}(X_{\varrho0}/X_{\varrho j})] C_1 + [X_{20} - X_{2j}(X_{\varrho0}/X_{\varrho j})] C_2 + \ldots + \qquad [16]$$

$$[X_{\varrho-1,0} - X_{\varrho-1,j}(X_{\varrho0}/X_{\varrho j})] C_{\varrho-1} + [X_{\varrho+1,0} - X_{\varrho+1,j}(X_{\varrho0}/X_{\varrho j})]$$

$$C_{\varrho+1} + \ldots + [X_{m0} - X_{mj}(X_{\varrho0}/X_{\varrho j})] C_m = Z_0 - (X_{\varrho0}/X_{\varrho j})Z_j.$$

By adding the terms $X_{\varrho0}C_j/X_{\varrho j}$ to both sides of equation 16, then the following is obtained:

$$[X_{10} - X_{1j}(X_{\varrho0}/X_{\varrho j})] C_1 + [X_{20} - X_{2j}(X_{\varrho0}/X_{\varrho j})] C_2 + \ldots + \qquad [17]$$

$$[X_{\varrho-1,0} - X_{\varrho-1,j}(X_{\varrho0}/X_{\varrho j})] C_{\varrho-1} + [X_{\varrho+1,0} - X_{\varrho+1,j}(X_{\varrho0}/X_{\varrho j})]$$

$$C_{\varrho+1} + \ldots + [X_{m0} - X_{mj}(X_{\varrho0}/X_{\varrho j})] C_m + (X_{\varrho0}/X_{\varrho j})C_j = Z_0 -$$

$$(X_{\varrho0}/X_{\varrho j}) (Z_j - C_j).$$

Note: Equation 17 is the expression for the objective function that corresponds to the extreme point associated with the new basis vectors given by equation 7.

It has already been observed that all of the coefficients $[X_{i0} - X_{ij}(X_{\varrho0}/X_{\varrho j})]$ in equation 17 must be positive if they are to be components of an extreme point of a convex set. With this in mind, equation 17 shows that *the new value of the objective function, obtained by replacing one of the vectors in the original basis, has a value less than the original objective function if* $Z_j - C_j > 0$ *and* $X_{\varrho j} > 0$. Now vectors $\check{P}_j$ can be chosen to enter the basis as long as $Z_j - C_j > 0$ for each j. In this way, the value of the objective function is decreased successively. This procedure can be continued until the situation $Z_j - C_j \leqslant 0$ for all remaining j; at this point the objective function will be minimized, subject to the given constraints and nonnegativity conditions, and thus the problem is solved.

APPENDIX 2:
LINEAR PROGRAMMING METHODS
FOR PRODUCTION SCHEDULING

Consider a company that manufactures automobile windshields. The sales department received orders (demands) for windshields for the next four months.

Month, i	January, 1	February 2	March, 3	April, 4
Unit prod. costs, c_i	$10	$12	$12	$10
Unit holding costs, h_i	$ 1.50	$ 2.00	$ 1.50	–
Demands, d_i	400	500	500	600

Note: The company presently has no windshields, $I_0 = 0$, and it is certain that no further orders will be received, $I_4 = 0$. In other words, I_N can be set at any desired level, say $I_N = 0$, to reduce inventory levels.

First, consider two extreme production policies (schedules):

Policy 1: Produce all 2000 windshields ordered in January (during the first month). $P_1 = 2000, P_2 = 0, P_3 = 0, P_4 = 0$ (amounts to produce), $I_1 = 1600, I_2 = 1100, I_3 = 600, I_4 = 0$ (inventory levels). Total cost = $25,500 = $20,000 production costs + $5,500 inventory costs.

Policy 2: Produce exactly the quantity of windshields ordered for that month (produce only to meet demand, that is, just in time). $P_1 = 400, P_2 = 500, P_3 = 500, P_4 = 600$ (amount to product), $I_1 = 0$,

$I_2 = 0$, $I_3 = 0$, $I_4 = 0$ (inventory levels). Total cost = \$22,000 = \$22,000 production costs + \$0 inventory costs.

Now, consider a third production policy:

Policy 3: Produce the quantity of windshields according to the following linear programming model:

$$\text{minimize:} \quad \text{T.C.} = 10P_1 + 12P_3 + 10P_4 + 1.5I_1 + 2I_2 + 1.5I_3$$

$$\text{subject to:} \quad P_1 - I_1 \quad\quad = 400$$

$$P_2 + I_1 - I_2 = 500$$

$$P_3 + I_2 - I_3 = 500$$

$$P_4 + I_3 \quad\quad = 600$$

$$\text{and} \quad P_1, P_2, P_3, P_4, I_1, I_2, I_3 \geqslant 0.$$

If this model is solved, then the best (optimal) solution is: $P_1 = 900$, $P_2 = 0$, $P_3 = 500$, $P_4 = 600$ (amounts to produce), $I_1 = 500$, $I_2 = 0$, $I_3 = 0$, $I_4 = 0$ (inventory levels). Total cost = \$21,750 = \$21,000 production costs + \$750 inventory costs.

Note: The total cost is less than either policy 1 or policy 2 as it balances production and inventory costs while meeting demand.

Asset Management Control Policies

How many items must be built in each time period to minimize the total cost over a planning horizon (several time periods)? We must satisfy all customer demands (orders).

$$I_0 \; P_1 \; d_1 \; I_1 \quad\quad I_{i-1} \; P_i \; d_i \; I_i \quad\quad I_{N-1} \; P_N \; d_N \; I_N$$

| period 1 | ... | period i | ... | period N |

In period i, I_{i-1} is the number of units of product on hand at the start of period i (entering inventory), P_i is the number of units produced (or purchased), and d_i is the number of units demanded, so that $I_i = I_{i-1} + P_i - d_i$.

This means that for demand to be met, the ending inventory equals the entering inventory plus the amount produced minus the amount demanded. The total cost to be minimized includes production and inventory costs. Total cost = total production costs + total inventory costs = $(c_1 P_1 + \ldots + c_N P_N) + (h_1 I_1 + \ldots + h_N I_N)$. c_i is the cost of manufacturing (or purchasing) *one unit* of the product during period i, and h_i is the cost of holding one unit of inventory durind period i.

To minimize total costs while meeting demand the problem is

minimize: $\text{T.C.} = c_1 P_1 + \ldots + c_N P_N + h_1 I_1 + \ldots + h_N I_N$

subject to:

$$P_1 - I_1 = d_1 - I_0 \quad \text{(period 1)}$$

$$P_2 + I_1 - I_2 = d_2 \quad \text{(period 2)}$$

$$\vdots \qquad \vdots \qquad \vdots$$

$$P_i + I_{i-1} - I_i = d_i \quad \text{(period i)}$$

$$\vdots \qquad \vdots \qquad \vdots$$

$$P_N + I_{N-1} - I_N = d_N \quad \text{(period N)}$$

$$P_1, P_2, \ldots, P_i, \ldots, P_N, I_1, I_2, \ldots, I_i, \ldots, I_N \geqslant 0.$$

This basic model (BM) is a linear programming model that can be solved by efficient methods once the demands (d_i) unit production costs (c_i) and unit inventory costs (h_i) are known. The model can be expanded to analyze several additional considerations. The model is a multiperiod production and inventory planning model that is useful for planning purposes for any length of time and over as many time periods (N) as desired. The solution method allows for analyzing changes in the demands, unit production costs, and the unit inventory holding costs.

The Production Smoothing Model

In our BM example, the fluctuating production schedule for January-April of $P_1 = 900, P_2 = 0, P_3 = 500$, and $P_4 = 600$ (batch production) may be very expensive, especially if significant amounts of resources (machinery or personnel) are committed to the product. Some reasons for high costs are overtime costs in months of high production (January) and costs associated with an idle work force in months of low production (February).

Balancing the production and inventory costs against the costs resulting from fluctuations tends to reduce the fluctuations in the resulting optimal production schedule. This type of optimal schedule is due to *production smoothing*. Consider the following policy example.

Policy 4: Produce exactly the same number of windshields each month. $P_1 = 500, P_2 = 500, P_3 = 500, P_4 = 500$ (amounts to produce), $I_1 = 100$, $I_2 = 100$, $I_3 = 100$, $I_4 = 0$ (inventory levels). Total cost = \$22,500 = \$22,000 production costs + \$500 inventory costs.

The Fixed Workforce Model

In order to provide a model that smooths production but allows for being able to measure cost coefficients in the smoothing terms, consider the Fixed Workforce Model (FWM), where production rates can be fluctuated only by utilizing overtime from the regular workforce (hiring and firing to absorb demand fluctuations are not allowed).

Note: Later, in the Variable Workforce Model (VWM), hiring and firing decisions will be allowed so that the total cost (TC) will include hiring and firing costs.

The general FWM is:

$$\text{minimize} \quad TC = (c_1 P_1 + \ldots + c_N P_N) + (h_1 I_1 + \ldots + h_N I_N) +$$

$$(r_1 R_1 + \ldots + r_N R_N) + (o_1 O_1 + \ldots + o_N O_N)$$

subject to:

$$P_i + I_{i-1} - I_i = d_i, \quad i = 1, \ldots, N \quad \text{(production-inventory balance equations)}$$

$$k_i P_i = R_i + O_i \quad , \quad i = 1, \ldots, N \quad \text{(total manpower equations)}$$

$$0 \leqslant R_i \leqslant (rm)_i \quad , \quad i = 1, \ldots, N \quad \text{(bounds on regular time man-hours)}$$

$$0 \leqslant O_i \leqslant (om)_i \quad , \quad i = 1, \ldots, N \quad \text{(bounds on overtime man-hours)}$$

$$P_i \geqslant 0, \ I_i \geqslant 0 \quad , \quad i = 1, \ldots, N \quad \text{(nonnegativity constraints)}$$

The new variables in (FWM) are R_i and O_i. The variables R_i represent the number of *regular time* man-hours of labor used during period i, and the variables O_i represent the number of man-hours of *overtime* labor used during period i. Also, the coefficients r_i represent the cost per man-hour of regular labor used in period i and the coefficients o_i represent the cost per man-hour of overtime labor in period i. Next, k_i represents the number of man-hours required to produce a single unit of product in period i (expected to decrease with time due to learning curve effects). Finally, $(rm)_i$ is the total number of man-hours of regular time labor available in period i and $(om)_i$ is the total number of man-hours of overtime labor available in period i.

Note: If r_i and o_i represent man-hours of direct production labor used in producing the product, then c_i represents all other costs (including material costs and indirect labor costs) in the production of a single unit of product during period i. Also, it may be of interest to have c_i only represent material costs and omit indirect costs.

The inventory holding costs, h_i, consist of the cost of capital tied up in inventory, storage costs, insurance costs, taxes, spoilage costs, and obsolescence costs (if any).

total costs = total production costs + total inventory costs

where

$$\text{total production costs} = (c_1 P_1 + \ldots + c_N P_N) + (r_1 R_1 + \ldots + r_N R_N) + $$
$$(o_1 O_1 + \ldots + o_N O_N)$$

and

$$\text{total inventory costs} = (h_1 I_1 + \ldots + h_N I_N)$$

It is clear that the total production cost in the FWM is different from that in the BM. However, if c_i is the unit material cost, r_i the direct regular time cost of one man-hour of labor, and o_i direct overtime cost of one man-hour of labor, then the FWM clarifies the issue of unit production costs as compared to the BM.

The *production-inventory balance equations* are the same as in the BM. The *total manpower equations* state that the number of man-hours required to produce a single unit of product in period i *times* the number of units of product produced in period i *equals* the number of man-hours of regular time labor in period i plus the number of man-hours of overtime labor in period i. In addition, the *bound inequalities* provide lower and upper bounds on the use of regular and overtime man-hours in each time period.

Note: An additional type of constraint can be augmented to FWM:

$$I_i \leq (sc)_i, \quad i = 1, \ldots, N$$

This constraint says that in period i the inventory (I_i) cannot exceed the storage capacity, $(sc)_i$.

The Variable Workforce Model

Whenever changing the workforce during the planning horizon is reasonable to counteract demand fluctuations, then the composition of the workforce becomes a decision variable whose values can change by hiring and firing workers. Also, the VWM allows for shortages to be included so that a back-ordering cost is part of the VWM.

The additional variables in this formulation are: H_i, the number of man-hours of regular workforce hired in period i; F_i, the number of man-hours of regular workforce fired in period i; I_i^+, the number of units of inventory carried in period i; and I_i^-, the number of units behind schedule in period i.

The associated costs with the above variables are: $h_i I_i^+$, the inventory holding cost in period i; $b_i I_i^-$, the back order (loss of good will) cost in period i; $e_i H_i$, the hiring cost in period i; $f_i F_i$, the firing cost in period i.

The general Variable Workforce Model:

$$\text{minimize } TC = (c_1 P_1 + \ldots + c_N P_N) + (h_1 I_1^+ + \ldots + h_N I_N^+) +$$
$$(b_1 I_1^- + \ldots + b_N I_N^-) + (r_1 R_1 + \ldots + r_N R_N) +$$
$$(o_1 O_1 + \ldots + o_N O_N) + (e_1 H_1 + \ldots + e_N H_N) +$$
$$(f_1 F_1 + \ldots + f_N F_N)$$

subject to:

$$P_i + I_{i-1}^+ - I_{i-1}^- - I_i^+ + I_i^- = d_i, \quad i = 1, \ldots, N \text{ (production-inventory balance equations)}$$

$$k_i P_i \leqslant R_i + O_i \qquad , i = 1, \ldots, N \text{ (total manpower)}$$

$$R_i - R_{i-1} = H_i - F_i \qquad , i = 1, \ldots, N \text{ (change in workforce in a period)}$$

$$O_i \leqslant p R_i \qquad , i = 1, \ldots, N \text{ (overtime bound as percentage of regular time)}$$

$$P_i, \ I_i^+, \ I_i^-, \ R_i, \ H_i, \ F_i \geqslant 0 \quad , i = 1, \ldots, N \text{ (nonnegativity constraints)}$$

Observe that the production-inventory balance equations are the same as before because $I_i = I_i^+ - I_i^-$ and $I_{i-1} = I_{i-1}^+ - I_{i-1}^-$.

I_i is positive if I_i^+ is positive and I_i is negative if I_i^- is positive (either $I_i^+ = 0$, or $I_i^- = 0$, both cannot simultaneously be positive). When I_i^+ is positive, there is an accumulation of back orders at the end of period i.

The total manpower relations limit production to available manpower. The change in workforce during a period's equations show that the regular workforce from period i−1 to period i equals the number hired minus the number fired during period i. Here, labor has been added in period i if H_i is positive or labor has been subtracted in period i if F_i is positive. Again, because there is a cost associated with both hiring and firing, both H_i and F_i cannot simultaneously be positive. Finally, the overtime bound as a percentage of the regular workforce just gives the total overtime available in period i as a function of the regular workforce size, where p is a percentage (i.e., $0 \leqslant p \leqslant 1$).

REFERENCES

BAZARAA, M. S. and J. J. JARVIS (1977) Linear Programming and Network Flows. New York: John Wiley.

BEIGHTLER, C. D., D. T. PHILLIPS, and D. WILDE (1979) Foundations of Optimization (2nd ed.). Englewood Cliffs, NJ: Prentice-Hall.

CHARNES, A. and W. W. COOPER (1961) Management Models and Industrial Applications of Linear Programming, vol. 1. New York: John Wiley.

DAELLENBACH, H. G., T. A. GEORGE, and D. C. McNICKLE (1983) Introduction to Operations Research Techniques (2nd ed.). Boston: Allyn and Bacon.

DANTZIG, G. B. (1963) Linear Programming and Extensions. Princeton, NJ: Princeton University Press.

ELMAGHRABY, S. (1966) The Design of Production Systems. New York: Rheinhold.

FORD, L. R. and D. R. FULKERSON (1977) Flows in Networks. Princeton, NJ: Princeton University Press.

GEOFFRION, A. M. [ed.] (1972) Perspectives on Optimization: A Collection of Expository Articles. Reading, MA: Addison-Wesley.

GARFINKEL, R. S. and G. L. NEMHAUSER (1970) "Optimal political districting by implicit enumeration techniques." Management Science 16, 8: B495-B508.

———(1972) Integer Programming. New York: John Wiley.

GASS, S. I. (1975) Linear Programming (4th ed.). New York: McGraw-Hill.

HADLEY, G. (1962) Linear Programming. Reading, MA: Addison-Wesley.

HILLIER, F. S. and G. J. LIEBERMANN (1975) Introduction to Operations Research (2nd ed.). San Francisco: Holden-Day.

HOLZMAN, A. G. (1981) "Linear programming," pp. 1-40 in A. G. Holzman (ed.) Mathematical Programming for Operations Researchers and Computer Scientists. New York: Dekker.

HU, T. C. (1969) Integer Programming and Network Flows. Reading, MA: Addison-Wesley.

IGNIZIO, J. P. (1976) Goal Programming and Extension. Lexington, MA: D. C. Heath.

JENSEN, P. and J. W. BARNES (1980) Network Flow Programming. New York: John Wiley.

KOLMAN, B. and R. E. BECK (1980) Elementary Linear Programming with Applications. New York: Academic Press.

LASDON, L. S. (1970) Optimization Theory for Large Systems. New York: Macmillan.

LAWRENCE, K. D. and S. H. ZANAKIS (1984) Production Planning and Scheduling: Mathematical Programming Applications. Industrial Engineering and Management Press.

LUENBERGER, D. G. (1984) Linear and Nonlinear Programming (2nd ed.). Reading, MA: Addison-Wesley.

ORCHARD-HAYES, W. (1968) Advanced Linear Programming Computing Techniques. New York: McGraw-Hill.

PHILLIPS, D. T., A. RAVINDRAN, and J. J. SOLBERG (1977) Operations Research: Principles and Practice. New York: John Wiley.

PLANE, D. R. and C. McMILLAN (1971) Discrete Optimization: Integer Programming and Network Analysis for Management Decisions. Englewood Cliffs, NJ: Prentice-Hall.

TAHA, H. A. (1975) Integer Programming: Theory, Applications, and Computations. New York: Academic.

———(1982) Operations Research: An Introduction (3rd ed.). New York: Macmillan.

von NEUMANN, J. and O. MORGENSTERN (1947) Theory of Games and Economic Behavior. Princeton, NJ: Princeton University Press.

WAGNER, H. M. (1975) Principles of Operations Research (2nd ed.). Englewood Cliffs, NJ: Prentice-Hall.

BRUCE R. FEIRING is currently a consultant and Adjunct Associate Professor of Management Sciences at the University of Minnesota. He has extensive academic and industry experience. Dr. Feiring was a Visiting Scientist of NASA, Johnson Space Center in Houston, Texas, and the Human Resource Laboratory, Brooks Air Force Base in San Antonio, Texas. He has written research publications on mathematical modeling, optimization, and control theory.

SAGE JOURNALS

The International Professional Publishers
2111 West Hillcrest Drive, Newbury Park, California 91320

S A G E
25
YEARS OF
INTERNATIONAL
PROFESSIONAL
PUBLISHING

Orders from the U.K., Europe, **Sage Publications, Ltd.**
the Middle East, and Africa 28 Banner Street
should be sent to: London EC1Y 8QE
ENGLAND

Orders from India and **Sage Publications**
South Asia should be sent to: **India Private Limited**
P.O. Box 4215
New Delhi 110 048 INDIA

These journals are available from Sage Periodicals Press.
See following pages for journals available from Sage, London.

ABSTRACTS IN SOCIAL GERONTOLOGY
Current Literature on Aging
Published in Cooperation with
The National Council on the Aging, Inc.
...provides abstracts and bibliographies of major articles, books, reports, and other materials on all aspects of gerontology: including demography, economics, family relations, government policy, health, institutional care, physiology, psychiatric dysfunctions, psychology, societal attitudes, work and retirement.
Quarterly: March, June, Sept., Dec. FIRST ISSUE: MARCH 1990
Yearly rates: Inst. $98 / Ind. $48 ISSN: 1047-4862

ADMINISTRATION & SOCIETY
Editor: Gary L. Wamsley,
Virginia Polytechnic Institute and State Univ.
...deals with administration, bureaucracy, public organization, and public policy — and the impact these have on politics and society.
Quarterly: May, Aug., Nov., Feb.
Yearly rates: Inst. $99 / Ind. $39 / ISSN: 0095-3997

AFFILIA: Journal of Women and Social Work
Editor-in-Chief: Betty Sancier, *Univ. of Wisconsin-Milwaukee*
...is a publication for and about women social workers and their clients. Its intent is to bring insight and knowledge to the field of social work from a feminist perspective and to provide the research and tools necessary to make significant changes and improvements in the delivery of social services.
Quarterly: Feb., May, Aug., Nov.
Yearly Rates: Inst. $64 / Ind. $30 / ISSN: 0886-1099

AMERICAN BEHAVIORAL SCIENTIST
...focuses, in theme-organized issues prepared under guest editors, on emerging cross-disciplinary interests, research, and problems in the social sciences.
Bimonthly: Sept., Nov., Jan., Mar., May, July
Yearly rates: Inst. $108 / Ind. $36 / ISSN: 0002-7642

AMERICAN POLITICS QUARTERLY
Editor: Susan Welch, *Univ. of Nebraska*
...promotes basic research in all areas of American political behavior — including urban, state, and national policies, as well as pressing social problems requiring political solutions.
Quarterly: Jan., April, July, Oct.
Yearly rates: Inst. $98 / Ind. $34 / ISSN: 0044-7803

THE ANNALS
of the **American Academy of Political and Social Science**
Editor: Richard D. Lambert
Associate Editor: Alan W. Heston
...Since 1891, The Annals has served as the preeminent forum for the interdisciplinary discussion of single problems and policy issues affecting America and the world community.
Bimonthly: Jan., March, May, July, Sept., Nov.
Yearly rates: Inst. $72 (p) / $89 (c) Ind. $32 (p) / $45 (c) ISSN: 0002-7162

BEHAVIOR MODIFICATION
Editors: Michel Hersen, *Western Psychiatric Inst. & Clinic*
Alan S. Bellack, *Medical College of Pennsylvania at EPPI*
...describes (in detail for replication purposes) assessment and modification techniques for problems in psychiatric, clinical, educational, and rehabilitational settings.
Quarterly: Jan., April, July, Oct.
Yearly rates: Inst. $100 / Ind. $38 / ISSN: 0145-4455

CHINA REPORT: A Journal of East Asian Studies
Editor: C.R.M. Rao,
Centre for the Study of Developing Societies, Delhi
...encourages the increased understanding of contemporary China and its East Asian neighbors, their cultures and ways of development, and their impact on India and other South Asian countries.
Quarterly: Feb., May, Aug., Nov.
Yearly rates: Inst. $59 / Ind. $30 / ISSN: 0009-4455

COMMUNICATION ABSTRACTS
Editor: Thomas F. Gordon, *Temple Univ.*
...provides coverage of recent literature in all areas of communication studies (both mass and interpersonal). Includes expanded coverage of new communications technologies.
Bimonthly: Feb., April, June, Aug., Oct., Dec.
Yearly rates: Inst. $270 / Ind. $90 / ISSN: 0162-2811

COMMUNICATION RESEARCH
Editor: Peter R. Monge, *Annenberg School, USC*
...provides an interdisciplinary forum for scholars and professionals to present new research in communication. Encourages rigorous studies of mass (and interpersonal) communication.
Bimonthly: Feb., April, June, Aug., Oct., Dec.
Yearly rates: Inst. $132 / Ind. $42 / ISSN: 0093-6502

COMPARATIVE POLITICAL STUDIES
Editor: James A. Caporaso, *Univ. of Washington*
...publishes theoretical and empirical research articles by scholars engaged in cross-national study, and includes research notes and review essays.
Quarterly: April, July, Oct, Jan.
Yearly rates: Inst. $96 / Ind. $32 / ISSN: 0010-4140

CONTRIBUTIONS TO INDIAN SOCIOLOGY
Editor: T. N. Madan, *Institute of Economic Growth, Delhi*
...a distinguished international forum for research on Indian and South Asian societies.
Biannually: May and November
Yearly rates: Inst. $59 / Ind. $27 / ISSN: 0069-9667

The COUNSELING PSYCHOLOGIST
Journal of Counseling Psychology
of the American Psychological Association (Div. 17)
Editor: Bruce R. Fretz, *Univ. of Maryland, College Park*
Editor-elect: Gerald Stone, *Univ. of Iowa*
...presents timely coverage — especially in new or developing areas of practice and research — of topics of immediate interest to counseling psychologists. Defines the field and communicates that identity to the profession as well as to those in other disciplines.
Quarterly: Jan., April, July, Oct.
Yearly rates: Inst. $90 / Ind. $32 / ISSN: 0011-0000

CRIME & DELINQUENCY
Published in cooperation with the
National Council on Crime and Delinquency
Editor: Don C. Gibbons, *Portland State Univ.*
...addresses specific policy or program implications or issues — social, political, and economic — of great topical interest to the professional with direct involvement in criminal justice.
Quarterly: Jan., April, July, Oct.
Yearly rates: Inst. $96 / Ind. $36 / ISSN: 0011-1287

CRIMINAL JUSTICE AND BEHAVIOR
Official Publication of the AACP
Published in affiliation with the ACA
Editor: Allen K. Hess, *Auburn Univ.*
...provides a means of communication among mental health professionals, behavioral scientists, researchers, and practitioners in the area of criminal justice.
Quarterly: March, June, Sept., Dec.
Yearly rates: Inst. $95 / Ind. $36 / ISSN: 0093-8548

Sage Periodicals Press A Division of SAGE Publications, Inc.
Newbury Park • London • New Delhi

ECONOMIC DEVELOPMENT QUARTERLY
The Journal of American Economic Revitalization
Editors: Richard D. Bingham, *Cleveland State*
Sammis B. White, *Univ. of Wisconsin-Milwaukee*
& Gail Garfield Schwartz, *NY State Public Serv. Commission*
. . .disseminates information on the latest research, programs, policies, and trends in the field of economic development. EDQ is unique in its concern for all areas of development — large cities, small towns, rural areas, and overseas trade and expansion.
Quarterly: Feb., May, Aug., Nov.
Yearly rates: Inst. $90 / Ind. $36 / ISSN: 0891-2424

EDUCATION and URBAN SOCIETY
. . .provides, through theme-organized issues prepared under guest editors, a forum for social scientific research on education as a social institution within urban environments, the politics of education, and educational institutions and processes as agents of social change.
Quarterly: Nov., Feb., May, Aug.
Yearly rates: Inst. $90 / Ind. $34 / ISSN: 0013-1245

EDUCATIONAL ADMINISTRATION ABSTRACTS
. . .provides abstracts drawn from more than 140 professional Journals relating to educational administration.
Quarterly: Jan., April, July, Oct.
Yearly rates: Inst. $188 / Ind. $66 / ISSN: 0013-1601

EDUCATIONAL ADMINISTRATION QUARTERLY
Published in cooperation with the
University Council for Educational Administration
Editor: Steven T. Bossert, *Univ. of Utah*
. . .seeks to stimulate critical thought and to disseminate the latest knowledge about research and practice in educational administration.
Quarterly: Feb., May, Aug., Nov.
Yearly rates: Inst. $90 / Ind. $36 / ISSN: 0013-161X

ENVIRONMENT AND BEHAVIOR
Published in cooperation with the
Environmental Design Research Association (edra)
Editor: Robert B. Bechtel, *Univ. of Arizona*
. . .reports rigorous experimental and theoretical work on the study, design, and control of the physical environment and its interaction with human behavioral systems.
Bimonthly: Jan., Mar., May, July, Sept., Nov.
Yearly rates: Inst. $120 / Ind. $48 / ISSN: 0013-9165

EVALUATION & THE HEALTH PROFESSIONS
Editor: R. Barker Bausell, *Univ. of Maryland*
. . .provides a forum for all health professionals interested or engaged in the development, implementation, and evaluation of health programs.
Quarterly: March, June, Sept., Dec.
Yearly rates: Inst. $96 / Ind. $36 / ISSN: 0163-2787

EVALUATION REVIEW
A Journal of Applied Social Research
Editors: Richard A. Berk & Howard E. Freeman,
both at Univ. of California, Los Angeles
. . .a forum for researchers, planners, and policymakers engaged in the development, implementation, and utilization of evaluation studies. Reflects a wide range of methodological and conceptual approaches to evaluation and its many applications.
Bimonthly: Feb., April, June, Aug., Oct., Dec.
Yearly rates: Inst. $120 / Ind. $45 / ISSN: 0193-841X

GENDER & SOCIETY
Official Publication of Sociologists for Women in Society
Editor: Judith Lorber,
Graduate School and Brooklyn College, CUNY
. . .focuses on the social and structural study of gender as a basic principle of the social order and as a primary social category. Emphasizing theory and research, G&S aims to advance both the study of gender and feminist scholarship.
Quarterly: March, June, Sept., Dec.
Yearly rates: Inst. $84 / Ind. $32 / ISSN: 0891-2432

GROUP & ORGANIZATION STUDIES
An International Journal
Editor: Michael J. Kavanagh, *SUNY, Albany*
. . .bridges the gap between research and practice for psychologists, group facilitators, educators, and consultants who are involved in the broad field of human relations training.
Quarterly: March, June, Sept., Dec.
Yearly rates: Inst. $100 / Ind. $42 / ISSN: 0364-1082

HISPANIC JOURNAL OF BEHAVIORAL SCIENCES
Editor: Amado M. Padilla, *Stanford University*
. . .publishes research articles, case histories, critical reviews and scholarly notes that are of theoretical interest or deal with methodological issues related to Hispanic populations.
Quarterly: Feb., May, Aug., Nov.
Yearly rates: Inst. $60 / Ind. $30 / ISSN: 0739-9863

HUMAN COMMUNICATION RESEARCH
Editor: James Bradac, *Univ. of Calif, Santa Barbara*
. . .publishes important research and high-quality reports that contribute to the expanding body of knowledge about human communication.
Quarterly: Sept., Dec., March, June
Yearly rates: Inst. $96 / Ind. $36 / ISSN: 0360-3989

HUMAN RESOURCES ABSTRACTS
. . .contains abstracts of the most important recent literature for the professional who needs easy reference to current and changing ideas in the diverse area of manpower and human resources development, and related social/governmental policy questions.
Quarterly: March, June, Sept., Dec.
Yearly rates: Inst. $188 / Ind. $66 / ISSN: 0099-2453

INDIAN ECONOMIC AND SOCIAL HISTORY REVIEW
Editor: Dharma M. Kumar, *Delhi School of Economics*
. . .focuses on the history, economy, and society of India and South Asia, and includes comparative studies of world development.
Quarterly: March, June, Sept., Dec.
Yearly rates: Inst. $70 / Ind. $35 / ISSN: 0019-4646

THE INDIAN JOURNAL OF SOCIAL SCIENCE
Sponsored by the Indian Council of Social Science Research
Editor: Sukhamoy Chakravarty, *Univ. of Delhi*
. . .promotes scientific discussion on the diverse concerns of social science research — the problems of development and social change, the interface between science, society, culture and technology, and a comprehension of future patterns of development as they relate to the developing countries.
Quarterly: March, June, Sept., Dec.
Yearly Rates: Inst. $59 / Ind. $35

INTERNATIONAL STUDIES
Editor: Anirudha Gupta, *School of International Studies, Jawaharlal Nehru Univ., New Delhi*
. . .the most outstanding Indian research journal in the field of international affairs and area studies.
Quarterly: Jan., April, July, Oct.
Yearly rates: Inst. $70 / Ind. $35 / ISSN: 0020-8817

JOURNAL OF ADOLESCENT RESEARCH
Editor: E. Ellen Thornburg, *Tucson, Arizona*
. . .provides professionals with the most current and relevant information on ways in which individuals ages 10-20 develop, behave, and are influenced by societal and cultural perspectives.
Quarterly: Jan., April, July, Oct.
Yearly Rates: Inst. $78 / Ind. $36 / ISSN: 0743-5584

JOURNAL OF AGING AND HEALTH
Editor: Kyriakos S. Markides,
Univ. of Texas Medical Branch, Galveston
. . .deals with social and behavioral factors related to aging and health, emphasizing health and quality of life.
Quarterly: Feb., May, Aug., Nov.
Yearly Rates: Inst. $78 / Ind. $36 / ISSN: 0898-2643

JOURNAL OF APPLIED GERONTOLOGY
The Official Journal of the Southern Gerontological Society
Editor: Miles Simpson, *North Carolina Central Univ.*
. . .strives to consistently publish articles in all subdisciplines of aging whose findings, conclusions, or suggestions have clear and sometimes immediate applicability to the problems encountered by older persons.
Quarterly: March, June, Sept., Dec.
Yearly rates: Inst. $88 / Ind. $38 / ISSN: 0733-4648

JOURNAL OF BLACK STUDIES
Editor: Molefi Kete Asante, *Temple Univ.*
. . .sustains full analytical discussion of economic, political, sociological, historical, literary, and philosophical issues related to persons of African descent.
Quarterly: Sept., Dec., March, June
Yearly rates: Inst. $92 / Ind. $34 / ISSN: 0021-9347

JOURNAL OF CONFLICT RESOLUTION
Journal of The Peace Science Society (International)
Editor: Bruce M. Russett, *Yale University*
. . .draws from interdisciplinary sources in its focus on the analysis of causes, prevention, and solution of international, domestic, and interpersonal conflicts.
Quarterly: March, June, Sept., Dec.
Yearly rates: Inst. $116 / Ind. $40 / ISSN: 0022-0027

JOURNAL OF CONTEMPORARY ETHNOGRAPHY
(formerly Urban Life)
Editors: Patricia Adler, *Univ of Colorado, Boulder*
& Peter Adler, *Univ. of Denver*
. . .the first journal dedicated to ethnography and qualitative
research in general. Advances sociological knowledge through
intensive, in-depth studies of human behavior in natural settings.
Quarterly: April, July, Oct., Jan.
Yearly rates: Inst. $105 / Ind. $34 / ISSN: 0891-2416

JOURNAL OF CROSS-CULTURAL PSYCHOLOGY
Published for the Center for Cross-Cultural Research,
Western Washington University
Editor: Juris G. Draguns, *Pennsylvania State Univ.*
Senior Editor: Walter J. Lonner, *Western Washington U.*
. . .presents behavioral and social research concentrating on
psychological phenomena as differentially conditioned by culture,
and on the individual as a member of the cultural group.
Quarterly: March, June, Sept., Dec.
Yearly rates: Inst. $94 / Ind. $35 / ISSN: 0022-0221

JOURNAL OF EARLY ADOLESCENCE
Editor: E. Ellen Thornburg, *Tucson, Arizona*
. . .provides a well-balanced, interdisciplinary, international
perspective on early adolescent development (age 10 through 14
years) and the factors affecting it.
Quarterly: Feb., May, Aug., Nov.
Yearly rates: Inst. $68 / Ind. $32 / ISSN: 0272-4316

JOURNAL OF FAMILY ISSUES
Sponsored by the National Council on Family Relations
Editor: Patricia A. Voydanoff, *Univ. of Dayton*
. . .devoted to contemporary social issues and social problems
related to marriage and family life, and to theoretical and professional issues of current interest to those who work with and study
families.
Quarterly: March, June, Sept., Dec.
Yearly rates: Inst. $95 / Ind. $35 / ISSN: 0192-513X

JOURNAL OF FAMILY PSYCHOLOGY
Journal of the Division of Family Psychology of the
American Psychological Association (Div. 43)
Editor: Howard A. Liddle, *Temple Univ.*
. . .enhances theory, research, and clinical practice in family
psychology and deals with: family and marital theory and concepts; research and evaluation; therapeutic frame works and
methods; training and supervision; policies and legal matters con-
cerning the family and marriage.
Quarterly: Sept., Dec., March, June
Yearly rates: Inst. $80 / Ind. $36 / ISSN: 0893-3200

JOURNAL OF HUMANISTIC PSYCHOLOGY
Published in cooperation with the
Association for Humanistic Psychology
Editor: Thomas Greening, *Psychological Service Associates*
. . .provides an interdisciplinary forum for contributions and con-
troversies in humanistic psychology as applied to personal growth,
interpersonal encounter, social problems, and philosophical
issues.
Quarterly: Jan, April, July, Oct.
Yearly rates: Inst. $90 / Ind. $34 / ISSN: 0022-1678

JOURNAL OF INTERPERSONAL VIOLENCE
Concerned with the Study and Treatment of Victims and
Perpetrators of Physical and Sexual Violence
Editor: Jon R. Conte, *Univ. of Chicago*
. . .provides a forum for discussion of the concerns and activities
of professionals and researchers working in domestic violence,
child sexual abuse, rape and sexual assault, physical child abuse,
and violent crime.
Quarterly: March, June, Sept., Dec.
Yearly rates: Inst. $80 / Ind. $35 / ISSN: 0886-2605

JOURNAL OF MENTAL HEALTH COUNSELING
Official Publication of the
American Mental Health Counselors Association
Editor: Lawrence Gerstein, *Ball State University*
. . .disseminates pertinent theory, therapeutic applications, and
research related to mental health counseling.
Quarterly: Jan., Apr., July, Oct.
Yearly rates: Inst. $60 / Ind. $26 / ISSN: 0193-1830

JOURNAL OF URBAN HISTORY
Editor: Blaine A. Brownell, *Univ. of Alabama, Birmingham*
. . .studies the history of cities and urban societies in all periods
of human history and in all geographical areas of the world.
Quarterly: Nov., Feb., May, Aug.
Yearly rates: Inst. $34 / Ind. $34 / ISSN: 0096-1442

JOURNAL OF RESEARCH IN CRIME AND DELINQUENCY
Published in Cooperation with the
National Council on Crime and Delinquency
Editor: Vincent O'Leary, *SUNY Albany*
. . .reports on original research in crime and delinquency, new
theory, and the critical analyses of theories and concepts especial-
ly pertinent to research development in this field.
Quarterly: Feb., May, Aug., Nov.
Yearly rates: Inst. $95 / Ind $36 / ISSN: 0022-4278

KNOWLEDGE:
Creation, Diffusion, Utilization
Editor: Robert Rich, *Univ. of Illinois*
. . .provides a forum for researchers, policymakers, R&D
managers, and practitioners engaged in the process of knowledge
development which includes the processes of creation, diffusion,
and utilization.
Quarterly: Sept., Dec., March, June
Yearly rates: Inst. $95 / Ind. $38 / ISSN: 0164-0259

LATIN AMERICAN PERSPECTIVES
A Journal on Capitalism and Socialism
Managing Editor: Ronald H. Chilcote,
Univ. of California, Riverside
. . .discusses and debates critical issues relating to capitalism,
imperialism, and socialism as they affect individuals, societies,
and nations throughout the Americas.
Quarterly: Jan., April, July, Oct.
Yearly rates: Inst. $95 / Ind. $32 / ISSN: 0094-582X

MANAGEMENT COMMUNICATION QUARTERLY
An International Journal
Editors: Paul C. Feingold, *USC*
Christine Kelly, *New York Univ.*
Larry R. Smeltzer, *Arizona State Univ.*
JoAnne Yates, *MIT*
. . .brings together communication research from a wide variety
of fields, with a focus on managerial and organizational effec-
tiveness. Includes book reviews and notes from professionals in
the field.
Quarterly: Aug., Nov., Feb., May
Yearly rates: Inst. $85 / Ind. $32 / ISSN: 0893-3189

MODERN CHINA
An International Quarterly of History and Social Science
Editor: Philip C. C. Huang, *Univ. of California, Los Angeles*
. . .encourages a new interdisciplinary scholarship and dialogue
on China's ongoing revolutionary experience.
Quarterly: Jan., April, July, Oct.
Yearly rates: Inst. $98 / Ind. $39 / ISSN: 0097-7004

PEACE & CHANGE
Sponsored by the Council on Peace Research in History
(CPRH) & the Consortium on Peace Research, Education and
Development (COPRED)
Editors: Robert D. Schulzinger & Paul Wehr,
University of Colorado-Boulder
. . .publishes scholarly and interpretive articles related to the
achieving of a peaceful, just, and humane society. It seeks to
transcend national, disciplinary, and occupational boundaries and
to build bridges between peace research, education, and action.
Quarterly: Jan., Apr., July, Oct.
Yearly rates: Inst. $60 / Ind. $30 / ISSN: 0149-0508

PERSONALITY AND SOCIAL PSYCHOLOGY BULLETIN
Journal of the Society for Personality and Social Psychology
Editor: Richard E. Petty, *Ohio State Univ.*
. . .publishes theoretical articles and empirical reports of research
in all areas of personality and social psychology.
Quarterly: March, June, Sept., Dec.
Yearly rates: Inst. $120 / Ind. $44 / ISSN: 0146-1672

PERSON-CENTERED REVIEW
An International Journal of Research, Theory, and Application
Editor: David J. Cain
. . .is devoted to the continued development of person-centered
theory, research, and application in the fields of psychotherapy,
education, supervision and training, and human development in
various group and organizational settings.
Quarterly: Feb., May, Aug., Nov.
Yearly rates: Inst. $80 / Ind. $35 / ISSN: 0883-2293

PHILOSOPHY OF THE SOCIAL SCIENCES
Editors: John O'Neill, I.C Jarvie,   New
J.N. Hattiangadi, J.O. Wisdom, *York University, Toronto*
. . .publishes articles, discussions, symposia, literature surveys,
and more of interest both to philosophers concerned with the
social sciences and to social scientists concerned with the
philosophical foundations of their subject.
Quarterly: March, June, Sept., Dec.
Yearly rates: Inst. $70 / Ind. $35 / ISSN: 0048-3931

POLITICAL THEORY
An International Journal of Political Philosophy
Editor: Tracy B. Strong, *Univ. of Calif., San Diego*
. . . provides a forum for the diverse orientations in the study of political ideas, including the history of political thought, modern theory, conceptual analysis, and polemic argumentation.
Quarterly: Feb., May, Aug., Nov.
Yearly rates: Inst. $98 / Ind. $35 / ISSN: 0090-5917

PSYCHOLOGY AND DEVELOPING SOCIETIES
A Journal Published by the Centre of Advanced Study in Psychology, Univ. of Allahabad, India
Chief Editor: Durganand Sinha, *National Fellow, Indian Council for Social Science Research, New Delhi,*
. . . provides a forum for psychologists from different parts of the world who are concerned with problems of developing societies. The journal will publish theoretical, empirical, and review papers which help to further understanding of the problems of these societies.
FIRST ISSUE: March, 1989 / Bi-Annual: March, Sept.
Yearly rates: Inst. $49 / Ind. $24

PUBLIC FINANCE QUARTERLY
Editor: J. Ronnie Davis, *Univ. of New Orleans—Lakefront*
. . . studies the theory, policy, and institutions related to the allocation, distribution, and stabilization functions within the public sector of the economy.
Quarterly: Jan., April, July, Oct.
Yearly rates: Inst. $115 / Ind. $44 / ISSN: 0048-5853

RATIONALITY AND SOCIETY
Editor: James S. Coleman, *University of Chicago*
. . . focuses on the growing contributions of rational-action based theory, and the questions and controversies surrounding this growth. The journal publishes work in social theory and social research based on the rational-action paradigm, as well as work challenging this paradigm.
First Issue, July 1989
2 issues in 1989: July, Oct. Quarterly in 1990
Rates: Inst. $141 / Ind. $57 (Vol 1&2-6 issues) / ISSN: 1043-4631

RESEARCH ON AGING
A Quarterly of Social Gerontology and Adult Development
Editors: Rhonda J.V. Montgomery, *Inst. of Gerontology, Wayne State Univ.*
& Edgar F. Borgatta, *Inst. on Aging, Univ. of Washington,*
. . . a journal of interdisciplinary research on current issues, methodological and research problems in the study of the aged.
Quarterly: March, June, Sept., Dec.
Yearly rates: Inst. $98 / Ind. $35 / ISSN: 0164-0275

SAGE FAMILY STUDIES ABSTRACTS
. . . abstracts major articles, reports, books and other materials on policy, theory, and research relating to the family, traditional and alternative lifestyles, therapy and counseling.
Quarterly: Feb., May, Aug., Nov.
Yearly rates: Inst. $188 / Ind. $66 / ISSN: 0164-0283

SAGE PUBLIC ADMINISTRATION ABSTRACTS
. . . publishes cross-indexed abstracts covering recent literature (plus related citations) on all aspects of public administration. Entries are drawn from books, articles, pamphlets, government publications, significant speeches, legislative research studies, and other fugitive material.
Quarterly: April, July, Oct., Jan.
Yearly rates: Inst. $188 / Ind. $66 / ISSN: 0094-6958

SAGE URBAN STUDIES ABSTRACTS
. . . publishes cross-indexed abstracts of important recent literature (plus related citations) on all aspects of urban studies: government and administration, policy, transportation, spatial analysis, planning, social analysis, community studies, education, finance and economics, law, management, environment, and comparative urban analysis.
Quarterly: Feb., May, Aug., Nov.
Yearly rates: Inst. $188 / Ind. $66 / ISSN: 0090-5747

SCIENCE, TECHNOLOGY, & HUMAN VALUES
Sponsored by the Society for Social Studies of Science (4S)
Editor: Susan E. Cozzens, *Rensselaer Polytechnic Institute*
. . . contains research and commentary on the development and dynamics of science and technology, including their involvement in politics, society, and culture.
Quarterly: Jan., Apr., July, Oct.
Yearly rates: Inst. $80 / Ind. $39 / ISSN: 0162-2439

SIMULATION & GAMING
An International Journal of Theory, Design, & Research
Official Journal of ABSEL, NASAGA, and ISAGA.
Editor: David Crookall, *Univ. of Alabama*
. . . publishes theoretical and empirical papers related to man, man-machine, and machine simulations of social processes; featured are theoretical papers about simulations in research and teaching, empirical studies, and technical papers on new gaming techniques.
Quarterly: March, June, Sept., Dec.
Yearly rates: Inst. $105 / Ind. $36 / ISSN: 1046-8781

SMALL GROUP RESEARCH
Name Change
An International Journal of Theory, Investigation, and Application (Incorporating Small Group Behavior and International Journal of Small Group Research)
Editors: Charles Garvin, *Univ. of Michigan and*
Richard Brian Polley, *Lewis & Clark College*
. . . presents research, theoretical advancements, and empirically supported applications with respect to all types of small groups. Through advancing the systematic study of small groups, this interdisciplinary journal seeks to increase communication among all who are professionally interested in group phenomena.
Quarterly: Feb., May, Aug. Nov.
Yearly rates: Inst. $98 / Ind. $38 / ISSN: 1046-4964

SMR/SOCIOLOGICAL METHODS AND RESEARCH
Editor: J. Scott Long, *Indiana Univ.*
. . . a leading journal of quantitative research and methodology in the social sciences.
Quarterly: Aug., Nov., Feb., May
Yearly rates: Inst. $100 / Ind. $38 / ISSN: 0049-1241

SOUTH ASIA JOURNAL
A Quarterly of the Indian Council for South Asian Cooperation
Editor: Professor Bimal Prasad, *School of International Studies, Jawaharlal Nehru Univ.*
. . . provides analyses of regional and national political, economic, historical, and cultural issues among the nations of South Asia.
Quarterly: July, Oct., Jan., April
Yearly rates: Inst. $65 / Ind. $30 / ISSN: 0970-4868

STUDIES IN HISTORY
Editor: S. Gopal, *Centre for Historical Studies, Jawaharlal Nehru Univ., New Delhi*
. . . reflects the expansion and diversification that has occurred in historical research in India in recent years.
Biannually: February and August
Yearly rates: Inst. $54 / Ind. $27 / ISSN: 0257-6430

URBAN AFFAIRS QUARTERLY
Editors: Dennis R. Judd and Donald Phares,
both at Univ. of Missouri, St. Louis
. . . emphasizes state-of-the-art research and scholarly analysis on urban themes: urban life, metropolitan systems, urban economic development, and urban policy. Historical and cross-cultural perspectives add to its interdisciplinary features.
Quarterly: Sept., Dec., March, June
Yearly rates: Inst. $96 / Ind. $34 / ISSN: 0042-0816

URBAN EDUCATION
Editor: Warren Button, *SUNY Buffalo*
. . . exists to improve the quality of urban education by making the results of relevant empirical and scholarly inquiry from a variety of fields more widely available.
Quarterly: April, July, Oct., Jan.
Yearly rates: Inst. $98 / Ind. 34 / ISSN: 0042-0859

WESTERN JOURNAL OF NURSING RESEARCH
A Forum for Communicating Nursing Research
Editor: Pamela J. Brink, *Univ. of Alberta*
. . . an innovative forum for scholarly debate, as well as for research and theoretical papers. Clinical studies have commentaries and rebuttals. Departments deal with current issues in nursing research.
Bimonthly: Feb., Apr., June, Aug., Oct., Dec.
Yearly rates: Inst. $108 / Ind. $48 ISSN: 0193-9459

WORK AND OCCUPATIONS
An International Sociological Journal
Editor: Curt Tausky, *Univ. of Massachusetts, Amherst*
. . . an international forum for sociological research and theory in the substantive areas of work, occupations, leisure — their structures and interrelationships.
Quarterly: Feb., May., Aug., Nov.
Yearly rates: Inst. $90 / Ind. $34 / ISSN: 0730-8884

WRITTEN COMMUNICATION
A Quarterly Journal of Research, Theory, & Application
Editors: Roger D. Cherry & Keith Walters, *Ohio State Univ.,* **and Stephen P. Witte**
. . . provides a forum for the free exchange of ideas, theoretical viewpoints, and methodological approaches that better define and further develop thought and practice in the exciting study of the written word.
Quarterly: Jan., April., July., Oct.
Yearly rates: Inst. $96 / Ind. $36 / ISSN: 0741-0883

YOUTH & SOCIETY
Editor: David Gottlieb, *Univ. of Houston*
. . . brings together interdisciplinary empirical studies and theoretical papers on the broad social and political implications of youth culture and development; concentration is primarily on the age span from mid-adolescence through young adulthood.
Quarterly: Sept., Dec., March., June
Yearly rates: Inst. $96 / Ind. $34 / ISSN: 0044-118X

Quantitative Applications in the Social Sciences

in the Social Sciences

(a Sage University Papers Series)

$7.50 each

SAGE PUBLICATIONS, INC.
P.O. BOX 5084
NEWBURY PARK, CALIFORNIA 91359—9924

Place
Stamp
here